NOT WITH A GUN

ALSO BY JEAN CARPER

Stay Alive!

Bitter Greetings: The Scandal of the Military Draft

The Dark Side of the Marketplace
(with Senator Warren G. Magnuson)

JEAN CARPER

NOT WITH A GUN

GROSSMAN PUBLISHERS

NEW YORK

1973

First published in 1973 by Grossman Publishers
625 Madison Avenue, New York, N. Y. 10022

Published simultaneously in Canada by
Fitzhenry and Whiteside, Ltd.

SBN 670-51673-2

Library of Congress Catalogue Card Number: 72-77704

Printed in U.S.A.

ACKNOWLEDGMENTS

I want to thank Seymour Glanzer, Assistant U.S. Attorney for the District of Columbia and U.S. Postal Inspector Jason Souder for their time in explaining to me how the fraud worked; a number of attorneys who talked with me, including Paul Pascal, Noel Thompson, John Rigby, and especially Maribeth Halloran and Norman Barnett of Neighborhood Legal Services. My gratitude, too, to the many Monarch customers who talked so openly to me; Judge Theodore Newman for his insights into the problem in general; Thea Flaum for her sensitive reaction to the manuscript as it was being written; Merle Gross and Freda Kharasch for their constructive comments on the final manuscript; my publisher Dick Grossman for his excellent revision suggestions and for seeing the possibilities of the book in the first place; and Max Weiner of Philadelphia, who had no direct connection with the book but who first opened my eyes to the horrors of these kinds of crimes against the poor.

I have not used the real names of certain individuals who have suffered from the practices described in this book wherever it seemed to me that to do so might add to their troubles.

J. C.

To Maribeth Halloran

"Now as through this world I ramble,
I see lots of funny men,
Some rob you with a sixgun,
And some with a fountain pen."
—Woodie Guthrie

During the summer of 1963 and on many nights and days thereafter until mid-1965, Nathan Herbert Cohen, with the unwitting help of many upstanding citizens in and around the District of Columbia, committed robbery. Not armed robbery that strikes and then is quickly forgotten, but robbery of a lingering and unforgettable kind that eats into people's lives like a cancer. This is the story of that crime.

NOT WITH A GUN

ON THE MORNING of June 28, 1965, one of those hot, muggy days in Washington, Woodrow Campbell, a black man, went to work as an air-conditioner installer in Silver Spring, Maryland, and his wife, Sarah, went to work as a maid in an Alexandria, Virginia, motel. Their daughter Margaret, age thirteen, youngest of five children, was home alone.

About eleven o'clock cars began lining up on the street and a crowd gathered in the yard. As Margaret looked on, bewildered, they pushed into the house. "They kept coming through the house, a whole crowd of them, looking everywhere, taking pictures of the house. I didn't know who they were. I thought maybe they were policemen searching the house. I was scared, so I called my mother at work. She told me to tell them to leave the house. I did, but they didn't pay any attention to me."

By the time Mrs. Campbell could get a bus from Virginia to the northeast section of Washington, it was all over. Their house had been sold at public auction. The crowd was gone.

It was nearly an hour before Woodrow Campbell's office got a radio message through to him in his truck. His son, working with him that summer, drove him home. Campbell was too dazed to do so.

For the next few months every time Campbell drove his truck up to a stoplight, he looked in the car next to him, hoping to see either Nathan Cohen or Myrvin Clark. "I really did. I won't lie about it. I was going to see who was the best man. I wasn't going to shoot him. I was going to beat him with my hands. Or I was going to try anyway."

*

President John F. Kennedy was still six months away from Dallas, Astronaut Gordon Cooper had just returned from circling the earth, the civil rights movement was still in its infancy—George Wallace had not yet made his stand at the schoolhouse door—and in Room 445 of the Cannon Building a conservative Texas Congressman, John P. Dowdy, whose only flamboyance was a ten-gallon white hat he liked to wear, was railing against the scandal of urban renewal in the District of Columbia—an ironic fact to be appreciated later—on that day, May 23, 1963, when the Monarch Construction Corporation was incorporated in the District of Columbia. One of the purposes of the company, as stated in the articles of incorporation, was home improvement: "To conduct and carry on the business of selling both retail and wholesale, without limit, any and all services, materials, products or by-products which enhance the value of land or buildings thereon."

Nathan Herbert Cohen, age twenty-six, had on that day probably never heard of Monarch. Listed as president of the new corporation was Paul J. McGarvey, a prematurely silver-haired Washington attorney who now styles himself a divorce lawyer. "I created that Frankenstein," he said recently of Monarch, "and when I met Mr. Frankenstein—er, I mean Mr. Cohen—I got out fast, as the records show. I was afraid to be associated with him." McGarvey claims the inspiration for

Monarch was another young attorney, Saul McGrane, a former classmate at the University of Maryland. McGrane, listed as one of the original officers and directors, agrees he drew up the incorporation papers, but says that the company was a mere shell, a nonoperating venture, until a few weeks after its inception, "Nate [as friends call him] bought out the company for the cost of incorporation, maybe five hundred dollars or so."

> Cohen: A big guy, must a weighed 275, and tall too—over six feet . . . a brilliant law student, took over his father's law practice after the old man died, didn't like it . . . comfortable family, lives high, chews a cigar. . . . Looks just like you see in the movies, those big fat gangsters, scared me a little . . . yeah, jus like Sydney Greenstreet . . . so fat when he come here he said he ought to sit on the floor. . . a genius. . . . an arrogant sonofabitch. . . . A mind like a calculating machine. . . . Contemptible. . . . A pitiful slob. . . . Just a fat overgrown kid . . . : These are some of the ways he was described by those who met him.

*

In the late spring of 1963 Nathan Cohen, a Baltimore businessman–lawyer who had practiced law for one year, in 1960–61, after his graduation with honors from the University of Maryland Law School, had just heard that a company he had once lent money to was in desperate financial difficulties. Cohen had a number of business interests, among them a family investment company, Consolidated Investment Corporation, which lent money to companies and bought stock. His mother, Thelma, his father-in-law, his brother-in-law, his wife's uncle plus a few outsiders, all had money in Consolidated.

The company in trouble was Custom Line Homes of Baltimore, maker of pre-fab houses, owned by Sam Abrams. Abrams reportedly asked Cohen to take Custom Line off his hands because he was so besieged by creditors that he was "ready to walk away from it." The company had heavy debts and few assets—except an idea that immediately appealed to Cohen. Abrams had blueprints for renovating old houses with what he called a "towne house front," a façade of aluminum siding, shutters, wrought-iron railing and lantern-type lights, reminiscent of the early 1900s. The attraction of the idea from an entrepreneur's viewpoint was that the "towne house front" gave a look of instant transformation without any expensive structural changes to the house, inside or out. The basic design could be altered with little trouble—by changing the trim or color of the aluminum—into about fifty different styles and quickly applied to the exteriors of entire neighborhoods of old row houses, which were in abundance in Washington, D. C. It was illusory renovation, but it was a dream Cohen felt would sell.

Cohen acquired the stock of Custom Line reportedly for "a nominal consideration." And the Cohen family enterprise, Consolidated Investment, picked up the "towne house front" plans from Custom Line for five thousand dollars.

Cohen, from his business and legal background, knew the intricacies of financing necessary to the success of merchandising the towne house fronts, but he was not a master salesman; at least he did not have the capabilities of setting up and operating a sales force on the scale his vision required. Soon after buying Custom Line, however, he began talking with an acquaintance, Saul McGrane, who generally operated in similar business circles. McGrane had done little with his fledgling company, the Monarch Construction Corporation, but he had come to know, in his words, "the world's super salesman," one Myrvin Cochran Clark, a Southerner of little education, who had been convicted in D.C. of home-improvement fraud in 1956. Clark, then forty-four, even bigger than Cohen, with dark wavy hair and a slightly pushed-in face, had the reputation of being able to talk anyone out of anything—even a jail sentence. After a seven-week nonjury trial in December 1956, in which Clark was found guilty of, among other misdeeds, forging promissory notes, he was given a suspended sentence of eight months to two years and put on probation. Clark, with two accomplices, had mulcted Washington homeowners of an estimated $250,000. Clark's attorney during the trial was John Croghan, a law partner of former Governor Harold Stassen.

One evening in the early summer of 1963 Clark and McGrane met at Cohen's home in Baltimore, along with Cohen's brother-in-law and business partner, Stanley Silver, an accountant married to Cohen's older sister, Harriet. As Silver recalled later, it was the first time he had ever heard of Monarch. "Clark and McGrane had the company, but it was not very active, and it was decided Nate and I were to get involved as prospective owners of Monarch." Monarch was to be used to merchandise the towne house front. Clark and McGrane were to stay on with the company, and McGarvey was to remain as president, at least for a while.

It must have seemed a perfect merger: Custom Line

Homes with its plans for the towne house front, and Monarch, complete with the selling talents of Myrvin C. Clark. But when Silver heard of Clark's previous conviction in home improvements—the very area they were to operate in—he was concerned. Cohen put him off, saying he had discussed the problem with Clark and Clark had promised not to repeat his mistake. Cohen was convinced, he said, that Clark was an excellent risk. Interestingly, Cohen, careful student that he was, claimed to have read the entire voluminous record of Clark's case, which contains explicit details of how the fraud was committed. Thus, when Cohen took to the streets as a salesman, as he eventually did, he was not entirely untutored. He had had one of the best teachers in the business, Myrvin C. Clark, the boy from Georgia turned professional con man.

> Cohen and Clark, the "two-ton Bobbsey twins," as they were called later by lawyers, cruising the streets of Washington, calling their office from the car phone. . . . Clark saying to his black victims, "Just call me Cee-gar Clark, that's right, Cee-gar Clark. You say you're from Georgia, Ah'm from Georgia maself." . . . We trusted him, we never done business with nobody like that before. They was just gangsters come in the night, come to rob us, only difference they didn't have a gun.

*

Cohen's initial investment in Monarch was not great—$10,000 he has said—but that gradually increased until he owned "a substantial share of the stock, more than 50 per cent." Stanley Silver also put in $10,000, and Cohen's mother, Thelma, invested about $40,000. Other capital came from "Nate's private investors," mainly a company known as the Richard Company in which Cohen and Silver also had money.

It was clear from the beginning that Cohen did not intend to act as a financier, leaving the daily management to someone else. He immediately moved the quarters of Monarch from a one-room shabby office in the District which McGrane had rented, to a seven-room suite of offices on the second floor of a high-rise building at 10111 Colesville Road, Woodmoor Shopping Center, in Silver Spring, Maryland, a suburb of Washington. He paid $6500 to have the offices remodeled and refurnished, and they were described as "lavish." It was Cohen's way of doing things, and consequently he was known as a man with money. In truth, according to family member Silver, Nathan in the years preceding Monarch had acquired very little money except through his wife Roseanne, who received a $100,000 inheritance from her grandfather. A financial statement for Nathan and Roseanne Cohen dated July 31, 1963, when Cohen was just getting Monarch in full swing, shows assets of $112,300, liabilities of $11,450, for a total net worth of $100,850. A statement of the same date for Silver and his wife shows a net worth of $112,000.

The Cohen family moved in on Monarch physically as well as financially. Every morning Nathan and his mother drove from Baltimore to Silver Spring. Eventually, they found the drive so tedious that Mrs. Cohen took an apartment in Silver Spring and Nathan moved his family to a house in Rockville, another D. C. suburb. Stanley Silver also began coming into the office regularly. Silver, a certified public accountant, was the general overseer of the finances and a party to the important decisions. Thelma, a small, not particularly pretty woman, described as a "tough businesswoman, domineering," kept the books and acted as office manager. There were no official directors' or officers' meetings. When a decision came up, the three of them, or sometimes the two of them—Nathan and his mother—talked it over themselves. Her influence over Cohen was apparent, even to the girls who worked in the office. They joked about Mrs. Cohen's coming in every day to look after her little boy Nathan. As it turned out, she emerged from Monarch two years later, unscathed, her $40,000 investment intact. Later, government prosecutors investigating Monarch never touched her, never called her before a grand jury, never interviewed her. Thus the extent of her participation in Monarch is unknown.

Cohen, although he came in with the modest title of assistant treasurer, acted as chief executive from the beginning, says McGrane. Both McGrane and McGarvey, original founders of Monarch, left the operation within a few months, although both continued to do legal work for the company for about a year, and McGarvey held the title of president until September 1, when Cohen took over in title as well as fact.

MCGRANE: Why did I leave? I didn't like the way it was going. Too much money was being paid out and nothing was coming in. You can't run a business like that. Cohen had money, though—at least he said he could get all the money he needed. I would say Cohen had the ability to raise money. But it would take a million dollars to do what they wanted to do. I often thought after that—before everything hit the fan—I just messed up on a real opportunity, here was a golden opportunity. All you had to do was pick up a paper and you saw all the jazz they had in there, all the advertising. But I'm glad as hell now I got out when I did.

What happened, in my opinion, I have no doubts in my mind it started out to be a very clean operation, but with not enough money behind you, you can't run an operation as big as they had planned, and it grew like Topsy, and ya gotta guy like Clark in there who is a top salesman. Clark does not believe in starting small. He would start with fifty salesmen. You've got to pay these people a draw. You've got to give them something to live on, and you can't do it without a lot of money behind you. If you've got fifty salesmen in there and give each of them a hundred dollars a week, that's five thousand dollars. This was Cohen's money. I think he got on a treadmill, and I have no doubts the salesmen put it over on him. I think the guy is painted a lot blacker than what he is. I think he got bad because he had to—circumstances.

Cohen and I have a falling out? No, the only falling out we had was when I told him he couldn't make it.

The silver-haired McGarvey, sitting with his feet on his desk, in his one-room law office with answering service, walls cracking and dirty, broken file cabinet, was eager to be exonerated. "You've seen Cohen. Tell me, would *you* want to meet that guy in a dark alley? Would *you* want to be associated in business with him? That's why I got out. Besides, Cohen was bringing in all those employees, and I knew that if he didn't pay their withholding taxes, the president of the corporation was responsible. That was me, and suppose in two or three years I'm left holding the bag for a couple of hundred thousand dollars in withholding taxes with Internal Revenue after me. They didn't want me in there anyway, me a little lawyer—I'm just small-time to them.

"Cohen was just a big fat—by the way you're not a Jew, are you?—well, he's a fat, arrogant, overstuffed Jew. A big-time operator—had to drive a Cadillac with a phone in it—you know the type, ostentatious. He's strictly show. If the Negroes knew then how he was raping their mothers—financially, I mean—they most likely would have killed him, but they didn't know.

"My conscience is clear. I got out early. You're not gonna say I was the instigator of Monarch, or anything, are you? I do a lot of work for the colored people now, divorce work—I don't want them to think I was tied up with it. I was just the president on paper. If you say I was the instigator behind Monach, I could sue you, you know."

During June and July Monarch geared up for its sales assault on Washington. Myrvin C. Clark took over as "executive manager," hired six sales managers and about fifty salesmen, whom he immediately promoted to "sales engineers." Clark, the showman and self-confessed hustler ("I've been a hustler all my life," he admits) trained the salesmen, held sales meetings every morning from nine until ten and a company-wide sales session once a month in the evening. Clark instructed salesmen in the psychological aspects of selling and often took salesmen out for demonstrations. They reported he had a nearly infallible memory, which led him to houses he had visited years ago during his hustling. One salesman tells how Clark, before entering, once described a house's interior and the woman who inhabited it, though he had not been there for years and she did not remember him. Clark stressed to salesmen that the single most important factor was the size of the monthly payment. If you could promise people a low monthly payment, they would buy, he insisted. It was true.

To obtain leads for Monarch's "sales engineers," Clark set up a "boiler room" of telephone solicitors on two shifts, one from 10 A.M. until 2 P.M., the other from 5 P.M., until 9 P.M. The solicitors, mostly women, each sat in a booth with headphone, calling selected areas of the inner city from a crisscross directory. It was their job to set up appointments for the "sales engineers who are going to be in your area next week." Additionally, Clark had a number of canvassers on the street looking for homes that needed repair. And to soften up prospects, Monarch made a mass mailing of postcards and folders, prepared by Clark. In that first month Monarch spent about $6000 on sales literature—pamphlets, film strips, photographs, blueprints, postcards, letters—all designed to create a desire for the "fabulous towne house front."

Sometime earlier Cohen and Clark had confined their focus to Washington's inner city—the near northwest, southeast, and northeast—with its streets of deteriorating row houses, and devised a remarkable concept that for a time cemented the appeal of their enterprise and gave it an aura of immense respectability. The towne house front plan was now called the "American Towne House Program—a Self-Help Urban Renewal Project." The linking of the decorative front with urban renewal was at once ingenious and insidious, for it made prospective Monarch customers, already worried about losing their homes to urban renewal (then a subject of dread among Washington blacks), more vulnerable and guaranteed the new program a certain amount of civic support. Who could be against a company that wanted to help poor people fix up their homes? The concept also, in a sense that Cohen, a man of style, acutely appreciated, elevated Monarch above the milieu of sleazy home-improvement contractors. Cohen, after all, was not a small-time salesman with holes in his shoes; he was a man of some means and considerable intelligence. Now with the advent of the American Towne House Program, he was also a civic benefactor.

From a Monarch booklet:

An Introduction to the American Towne House Program

The American Towne House Program itself is a new concept for revitalizing and saving existing neighborhoods, particularly row-house areas. The program is accomplished by designing, engineering, and installing new urban Towne House fronts individually for each row house and each homeowner through the utilization of modern building techniques and modern building materials; through the use of our own specially trained crews in conjunction with responsible subcontractors.

For Example: A single two-story old brick row house can be renovated into a new and exciting eighteenth-century Towne House or a modern twentieth-century Towne House by the replacement of old and obsolete large window panes with neat, new, small "six over six" window sash, and the installation of maintenance-free alu-

minum clapboard siding and aluminum shutters on the upper story and with a "Towne House" off-white or orange-red or charcoal brick stain on the bottom story, with beautiful wrought-iron "Towne House" wall lantern-lights next to the new, heavy "Towne House" door and trim, plus a concrete porch and steps with wrought-iron rails and pickets, and a transformation that approaches a minor miracle has actually occurred.

NOW: Multiply this one individually designed "Towne House" front by the number of houses in that block and the number of blocks in the "Towne House Section" with each house being individually designed, and then begin to visualize the enormity and scope of this "American Towne House Program."

Who "Profits" from the Towne House Program?

The Nation's Capital gains more from the success of the American Towne House Program than the individual homeowner or Monarch Construction Corporation. When the row house area from the White House and the Capitol to Allison Street in the northwest is changed from an old, run-down "row house" status to a new-look urban Towne House area, then this program has saved all the taxpayers millions and millions of dollars. For a row house area that has been going "downhill" for years and ends up as a slum area beyond repair is expensive to the city in terms of millions of dollars. This condition and environment is expensive in terms of health, education, family life, crime, and such sociological and psysiolog·cal [sic] deterioration that is uncountable in terms of monetary costs.

National and world-wide opinion of the District of Columbia and of the United States is partly based on the views of our visitors. These visitors travel through the resi-

dential areas of the District of Columbia. In front of our Nation's Capitol and in front of our White House is an area of old row houses in "slum" conditions or near "slum" conditions.

How expensive is this in terms of national pride?

How expensive is this in terms of world opinion?

How expensive is this in terms of our "Democracy"—Better-Way-of-Life-Sell to other nations?

The District of Columbia and all its taxpayers and our Nation profit from the American Towne House Program.

The Home Owner

As proved by the "Georgetown" and "Capitol Hill" projects [both Georgetown, now a wealthy section of Washington, and parts of Capitol Hill were once virtual slums and underwent extensive rehabilitation], town houses, even when constructed in gutted shells of former row houses have a value and demand far in excess of the original property value. Obviously, everyone in Northwest Washington cannot afford to spend $15,000 to convert their "row house" into a "Georgetown" urban towne house creation. However, most of the Towne House Section are row houses that are in much better condition than were the row houses in the slum areas of Georgetown and Capitol Hill. The American Towne House Program hinges on the fact that the transformation of these row house areas did bring about a substantial increase in property values. The homeowner does not spend $15,000 in the American Towne House Program. He only spends an average of $1500, and this amount is paid on a small monthly payment plan.

The American Towne House Program is geared for

volume production and installation. This saves the individual homeowner money.

The property values are enhanced in this area for the benefit of the existing homeowner.

The individual homeowner has all to gain and nothing to lose.

Good (morning/evening) (Mr./Mrs.) B. My name is Mr. ———. I'm with Monarch Construction Corporation and stopped by to see if you received our Towne House folder. Did you receive it? Good. . . . Like the Towne House folder said, you know what happened to the prices of real estate in Georgetown, Foggy Botton (another renovated area in Washington), and Capitol Hill. Just a few years back you could have bought houses in any of these areas for around twelve thousand dollars. Today you could not buy any of them for thirty thousand dollars, and you know why? It's because of the "Towne House" look, the newest thing in real-estate value-raising in the country. You have read in the papers where it is happening in Baltimore and Philadelphia. This is your chance of a lifetime to both beautify and raise the value of your home. Wouldn't you like to have the "Towne House" look? Wouldn't you like to raise the value of your home to thirty thousand dollars?

One of our sales engineers will be completing the details of the Towne House with several of your neighbors tomorrow evening. Don't you want to have him stop by your home for your once-in-a-lifetime Towne House? Good. What time will you and (Mrs./Mr.) be home?

When the salesmen began their walks up and down Washington streets, they carried sales kits containing photos of civic leaders who supposedly backed the American Towne House Self-Help Urban Renewal Program. Salesmen were instructed to show the photos and mention the names of prominent Negro leaders or others who "endorsed" the program. When investigators inspected Monarch's files, they found photos of the Reverend Channing Phillips, a black civic leader in Washington, Edith Throckmorton and the Rev. Dr. Edward Hailes of the NAACP, Kenneth Brown and William S. Brown, officials with the Federal Housing Administration (FHA), Doyle Mitchel, president of the Industrial National Bank, and Congressman John Dowdy with and without his white hat. (Dowdy was chairman of a subcommittee of the House District Committee, a well-known crime fighter and critic of public urban renewal.) All the photos had been taken in Monarch offices during sales meetings. Many of the civic leaders, salesmen said later, had spoken at sales meetings. Monarch then used their photos and taped speeches, without their knowledge, as an endorsement of the urban renewal towne house program.

Not unexpectedly, the urban renewal rhetoric soon began to obscure the fact that Monarch was a private, profit-making firm. Cleveland Reed, a former Monarch salesman, told a Congressional investigating committee in 1967 that the telephone solicitors even neglected to mention the name of Monarch. "They said something like: 'We are calling you from the American Towne House Program of self-help urban renewal, and we would like to send out an engineer to see you, to talk to you about upgrading the values of your property.'" Then, Reed said, he or another salesman would go to the house: "'Mrs. Jones, I am Cleveland Reed from the American Towne House Program. I have an appointment, I believe, to see you and Mr. Jones,' and just walk in." The pitch, said Reed, was calculated to create the impression the salesman was an urban renewal official or engineer with the D. C. government. Only if asked directly was a salesman to deny a government affiliation. This approach, Reed said, was encouraged by Clark.

By mid-July Monarch was fully ready to move, and Clark, apparently caught up in the spirit of the rhetoric he had helped invent, gave his salesmen periodic send-offs by signing all his correspondence to them with:

YOURS FOR A BETTER WASHINGTON!

*

At that point Monarch was not to be stopped, although in retrospect it might never have got underway—at least in the form it did—except for a wrong decision by a city official at an earlier, critical juncture. The District of Columbia requires licenses for both salesmen and home-improvement contractors. And although some salesmen operate without them, it was not a chance Cohen and Clark could afford to take because the size of their organization alone would thrust them into public view. Monarch's license was readily approved after a routine police check, but when the Special Investigations Branch of the D. C. Police Department, as was then the procedure, checked into Clark, they predictably ran across his previous conviction for home-improvement fraud, along with several other violations. He had been sued twenty-six times in court for debts and had judgments exceeding $45,000 outstanding against him. He had been arrested in 1951 and 1953 for being drunk (Clark is a self-admitted alcoholic) and forfeited $10 bail on both occasions. He also had been arrested in October 1961 for disorderly conduct.

Because of his bad record, the police department recommended against giving Clark a home-improvement salesman's license in 1963 and repeated its negative recommendations when his license came up for renewal in 1964 and 1965.

*

Julian Green, of the D. C. Department of Licenses and Inspections, in charge of granting such licenses, when questioned:

Mr. Green, how is it that you approved a license for Myrvin Clark when he had been convicted of home-improvement fraud in 1956?

He showed me to my satisfaction that he had a firm program of relieving himself of this impediment. He also had been approved by the FHA as a dealer, and he furnished me with some evidence as to his attempts to satisfy his indebtedness.

Did it worry you at all that he had been convicted of home-improvement fraud before?

Yes, but he had all kinds of recommendations, letters, and references.

Who were those from?

I don't recall now. I think one of them was from Senator Talmadge of Georgia. But I don't remember who the others were from. Clark was at the time a major in the United States Army Reserve; he had served with distinction in World War II and had many commendations. He was an administrator after the war in setting up the government in Germany.

So this was an action you took entirely on your own?

That's right. I was satisfied he was a trustworthy individual who was entitled to a license.

You must have found him impressive?

Oh, yes. I didn't find Cohen so impressive—he also came in to see me—but Clark, that's a different story. He must have taken a course with Dale Carnegie, he's a very winning individual, sure has a gift for gab, but that's probably why he was able to talk so many people into buying. I wonder what he's doing now. In California? I wouldn't be surprised to see him turn up in the movies.

Do you have any regrets about licensing Clark in light of what happened?

I guess you might say I do. I would say my faith in him was—uh—misplaced.

THE OWNERS of 313 Wade Street, N.W., were Grant Lee and Theresa Taylor, a young black couple, he thirty-three, she twenty-five, with six children. The Taylors were the kind of black family rarely written about in sociology studies. Theresa, a bouncy woman of great energy and warmth, was going back to school in between the births of her babies to learn to be a nurse. Taylor, the only child of a white-collar worker, was ambitious, reserved, a nondrinker, prompt payer of his debts, a protector of his family, a man better educated than most blacks, who believed in advancement through hard work. After high school graduation in D. C. he had taken night courses in business administration at Howard University, but found it didn't make any difference. "Blacks still couldn't get jobs at that time," he recalls. Finally he took a job as an animal caretaker at Walter Reed Medical Center in Bethesda and hoped things would get better. At the time Monarch sought him out he was making $5100 a year as a grade WB-5 and driving a cab at night.

In July 1963 a young salesman, still in college, John Garrison, who had been recruited by Clark at a junior chamber of commerce meeting a few weeks earlier, called on the Taylors. They had received Monarch literature in the mail and were only mildly interested. They already had heavy expenses: for the house, a secondhand car they had just bought, food and clothing for eight people, and Theresa's schooling. Nor was their house in particularly bad repair. Taylor was concerned about a leak that had recently appeared in the roof, but he planned to fix it himself. The red brick structure was sound. The Taylors had bought the house in 1957; it was the first house they had ever owned and they loved it. Theresa still keeps a faded, crumpled photograph of the house as it looked the day they bought it.

Garrison, though inexperienced, was persuasive. He showed them photos, illustrating how their house would look with a towne house front. The photos were handsome and reminded Theresa of the "Georgetown look." Garrison also said the front would increase the value of their home; the cost, they believed, would be about $1700.

Still the Taylors wavered over assuming a sizable new debt and, as they recall, probably would not have signed a contract had it not been for the appearance at the house of William Whitted, a tall, handsome, light-skinned Negro, who lived nearby and was Garrison's sales supervisor. Whitted, who now works at the Land Redevelopment Agency for the District of Columbia, is a man of astounding verbal abilities. "The words just rolled off his tongue," Taylor recalls. Whitted had been hired by Clark in one of the six top positions as sales manager; he was a valuable asset to Monarch, not only for his golden-tongue but also for his dark skin. Clark had tried unsuccessfully to stack the sales force with blacks. Whitted was one of his prizes. Understandably, the Taylors trusted him, a black man and a neighbor. "I figured he wouldn't cheat one of his own kind. But I guess he was after the money and didn't care."

Whitted, says Taylor, assured him their debts on the house would be consolidated so that a new monthly payment —even with the cost of the new front included—would be *less* than what they were then paying. And yes, they would fix the roof Taylor was worried about. For those living marginally the promise of a lower monthly obligation was Monarch's most powerful selling point, for not only would there be no immediate extra financial burden, but some money, then tied up in monthly payments, would be freed for other uses. It was an appealing offer to the Taylors, who, like others, were always short of extra money after each two-week paycheck.

Another compelling argument, Taylor remembers, was the frightening one concerning urban renewal. At that time Washington was in the midst of a vast urban renewal program, the largest of any city in the nation. Whole sections of old housing, notably in the southwest section, were being condemned, razed, and new apartment buildings were rising on the rubble. The "substandard" homes destroyed, of course, were those of blacks. No black could escape noticing the bulldozers, wreckers, the rising steel girders, or hearing the tales of misery about friends and relatives who had been "urban removed." Taylor, as a part-time cabdriver, daily drove by the wreckage and construction. So when a Monarch salesman told him he was in danger of losing his house to urban renewal unless he improved it, he saw no reason to disbelieve. He was also told, he recalls, that if the government did condemn his house, the new front would increase the value of the house, bringing a much higher condemnation price.

That night, July 18, Grant and Theresa Taylor signed a

contract, with Garrison noted as salesman. The early records of Monarch have been destroyed, but Garrison's copy of the contract along with a few other papers signed by the Taylors are still in existence. It appears from the records that the Taylors were Monarch's first customer: a tragic distinction, if it is true, marking an ominous beginning for Monarch.

The contract they signed called for:

1 towne house style 7 front	$1500
9 storm windows and 1 new back door—wood	200
new roof	275
1 basement partition	100
	$2075

The Taylors thought little more about the transaction until a few weeks later Nathan Cohen and a man named Earl Lapin came one evening to work out financing for the deal. Lapin, a native New Yorker who attended Princeton and graduated from George Washington University in 1949, struck the Taylors as more refined than Cohen, "a more sensible, dignified man who talked in a lower tone." Lapin represented himself as a real-estate broker-attorney, a disinterested party who had accompanied Cohen to arrange financing. Lapin, in fact, was not a lawyer—he had completed one year at George Washington University Law School—and he was not disinterested. Cohen had hired him at Monarch and then taken him off the payroll. Lapin, who had a real-estate broker's license and contacts in Washington banks, was then used to negotiate loans for Monarch customers, necessary to pay for the towne house fronts. Under the aegis of his one-man brokerage firm, Empire Realty Services, Inc., Lapin was to contact banks on behalf of customers to obtain new first mortgages, a common task for real-estate brokers. Under D. C. law, a real-estate broker has a special obligation—like a trustee—to look out for the interests of his client, the homeowner. Lapin's activities, on the other hand, benefited mostly Cohen and Monarch. It was a vital role, one that was to enrich Lapin and make him an important functionary in the Monarch operation.

The precise details of what happened that night are unclear from the records, but of importance is that the Taylors signed several papers. One was a new contract dated August 21, 1963, this time with Cohen listed as salesman. Scrawled in his handwriting, this one read differently:

> *Install American Towne House Front, including aluminum clapboard siding on entire front of house. Change windows for 6 over 6 sash. Install wrought-iron railings on front porch. Install Towne House door & trim. Furnish and install Towne House Lantern. Work includes plans, permits, etc. Work to start approximately 30 days, to be completed approximately 120 days.*
> *Total price for labor and materials $3475*
> *Balance payable upon completion of work $3900*
> *Owner to pay balance in equal installments of $65 each.*

The new contract called for no new roof or basement partition and the price had jumped from $2075 to $3900.

•

In December of that year, salesman John Garrison, who by that time had left Monarch, sued the company for his commission of $587 on the Taylor job. During the trial Judge John

J. Malloy questioned Nathan Cohen about the sharp rise in price in the rewritten contract. Cohen testified he had "run into trouble on the job and had to increase the price." It was the earliest clue on record to the secret of Cohen's operation, but it went unnoticed as nothing more than the plausible explanation of a legitimate businessman. Garrison did not get the commission; it went to William Whitted.

*

Additionally, without their knowledge, the Taylors signed, also that night, a promissory note for $3900 payable to Monarch, and, as security for that note, a mortgage on their home which in the District of Columbia is called a deed of trust. A deed of trust is identical to a mortgage except that, as a precaution against abuse, it must bear the names of two persons designated as "trustees." These trustees, in effect, hold the deed in trust until the debt secured by the mortgage is paid off, and have the power to foreclose on a home to satisfy the debt if necessary. The trustees were intended by the law to be disinterested parties representing both the homeowner and the lender. In practice, the trustees in the District are named by the lender—usually because of business ties—and are counted on to do his bidding to the detriment of the homeowner. Named as trustees on the Taylors' mortgage were Monarch employees William Whitted and Saul McGrane.

In December Lapin summoned the Taylors to his office and explained he needed them to sign more papers for the "financing." They did. "We thought he was our lawyer, working for us. When he said sign, we did." At Lapin's request the

Taylors put their signatures to a new first mortgage for $9000 with the Montgomery Federal Savings and Loan Association as well as another $3900 note payable to Monarch, also backed up by a mortgage. Lapin had promised the Taylors to consolidate their debts into a single payment of $60 or $70 monthly, and these documents were necessary to do so, he told them.

Of special consequence to the Taylors was the $3900 note signed in December, for as it turned out, Lapin himself acquired the note from Cohen—at what price is unknown—and thus the Taylors now were obligated under the terms of the note to send Lapin $65 monthly. As assurance they would, Lapin also held the second mortgage, with himself and a business acquaintance, Eugene P. Alexander, listed as trustees. Such an action was a departure from Lapin's usual procedure; he often was named as a trustee, but ordinarily he did not buy promissory notes from Monarch; he acted merely as a real-estate broker negotiating the loans. As far as can be determined, the Taylors' note was the only one he bought from Monarch.

Before their encounter with Monarch the Taylors owed $7000 on their home and were due to pay it off in 1969. Afterward, according to the Recorder of Deeds office, they owed three mortgages totaling $16,800 plus interest (which over the years would increase the debt to more than $25,000), although they never realized the extent of their indebtedness until so informed eight years later. All the Taylors knew in 1964 was that to their bewilderment they were struggling against an unmovable mountain of debt. Instead of the single low monthly payment Lapin had promised, they were now encumbered with three separate house payments amounting to nearly $200. This, combined with their monthly car payment of $50 and other commitments, such as insurance and taxes, nearly depleted Taylor's monthly take-home pay of $380. The Taylors could not understand how it had happened, but they did know that until they could get the matter straightened out, they would have to keep paying.

Monarch workers did come and put on the front, but to the Taylors it looked tinny and cheap, unlike the glamorous pictures. The workmen refused to repair the roof or honor the other commitments made in the original $2000 contract—which the Taylors no longer even possessed. As was his practice, Cohen, unknown to them, had taken it and destroyed it.

Taylor tried to juggle his debts, paying one creditor one month, another the next, all the while trying to explain it was a mix-up. It was just supposed to be one small payment, Earl Lapin had said. Taylor sank further behind. He was harassed at work by phone calls from creditors. They called him; they called his supervisor, who begged him to try to pay off his bills. Taylor, who had worked at Walter Reed for ten years, grew fearful of losing his job. He couldn't concentrate on his work, and his supervisor became increasingly irritated by the interruptions. Taylor's first act when he came home at night was to lift the phone from the hook to stop the abusive rings. Theresa cried at night. The children were upset. Taylor drove the cab more often now, all day Saturday and Sunday also; it was the only money they had for food.

Taylor remarkably managed to make payments continuously enough to fend off his creditors throughout all of 1964.

But by early 1965 Earl Lapin, noteholder and trustee, had become increasingly impatient. Taylor was delinquent with several payments. Taylor paid Lapin $65 in January and $65 in February. It was the last payment he was ever to make to Lapin, except the final forfeiture. Sometime in May, Lapin placed a phone call to Adam Weschler & Son, auctioneers. Lapin then wrote a letter to the Taylors stating the date on which they must be off the premises. He was planning to foreclose.

Under District law, foreclosure is a fairly automatic procedure. The noteholder requests the trustee to foreclose—in this case, Lapin acted in both capacities—who then notifies the auctioneer to proceed as required by law. The auctioneer, who receives a commission or fee from the sale, then must advertise the property for ten days in a local paper. Ordinarily, no check is made on the validity of the note or the debt. In this case Weschler knew Lapin, and his call was enough to put the foreclosure procedure in operation. It could not be stopped without a court order or contravening instructions from Lapin.

Grant and Theresa Taylor, when they received the letter, were disbelieving. As quickly as they could they went to find a lawyer. They went to Legal Aid, the counseling service for the poor operated by the D. C. Bar Association. Whatever the technicalities of the lawyer's advice, it followed the sanctity of signatures on promissory notes. He advised the Taylors that, since they had signed the note, their only recourse was to pay—or lose their home. He did not suggest any other remedies, such as seeking a temporary restraining order to stay the auction until the Taylors could make a defense in court, a technique later used by more aggressive lawyers with Monarch cases.

Grant Taylor was desperate, but he still believed Lapin was a decent man. Taylor, as was his character, blamed himself mostly for being misled into deep debt. He was ashamed that he, a man who had studied business administration, was so incompetent in handling his own affairs. Until that time he had told few persons of his business difficulty. No one at work, nor even his close relatives, knew the real nature of it. Now, in panic, taking the lawyer's advice, he went to his father to borrow money. He went to Theresa's father, to her uncle. He scraped up nearly $500 in cash; he calculated he was about seven payments behind to Lapin, but he wasn't sure. Now Taylor, who had avoided the phone, was on it constantly to Lapin's office. Mr. Lapin wasn't in. "No, I don't know when to expect him. No, he is *not* in. This is his answering service."

Taylor was determined to find Lapin. That Saturday morning after his visit to Legal Aid, he and Theresa took the bus to Lapin's office in an old building across from the Government Printing Office about three blocks from the Capitol. Theresa remembers they had to pass by some rubble downstairs to get to the second-floor office. They had planned to get Lapin at a time when he didn't expect them and couldn't put them off. They were right. When they walked in, he was at his desk going through some papers. He looked up, surprised to see them, explained that he rarely came in on Saturday and that his secretary wasn't there. As they recall, he began speaking in a sympathetic way, expressing regret over what he had had to do.

"He kept talking, saying he needed the money for this and that." Taylor interrupted, asking exactly how much they were behind. Lapin told them—about $460, as the Taylors recall. Taylor then took the cash from his pocket and counted it out on the desk. "Well, there it is." For an instant the Taylors did not believe Lapin had seen it. He kept offering excuses, kept talking. And then Theresa saw him harden into a man she had never seen before. His words stick vividly in her mind: "No. Under no circumstances." Taylor recalls that he went on arguing with Lapin, who raised the ante. He then insisted on not only the back payments but also next month's payment of $65, which Taylor didn't have. For the first time it occurred to Taylor that Lapin was not an independent lawyer, honestly trying to help them, but was "in with Monarch." Finally, the Taylors gave up and went home to the only consequences that seemed possible. They packed up their goods and prepared to move out.

*

Theresa began having nightmares and headaches. "Sleep was impossible, maybe catch a wink here or there, and the *dreams.* You know you just can't sleep. You have these terrible dreams and nightmares, wondering what are you going to do, where are you going, how are you going to manage with six kids and nowhere to go. We tried everything, and we didn't get any help. None whatsoever—they just turned us away. I don't even like to remember it—it's a part of my life I've just tried to cut out."

Taylor, raised a Baptist, went to see a priest.

The following Thursday, May 27, this advertisement appeared in the classified section of the Washington *Evening Star*:

ADAM A. WESCHLER & SON
Trustees sale of valuable 2-story row brick dwelling, No. 313 Wade St., N.W. Full basement, gas, hot water heat.

By virtue of a deed of trust recorded in Liber N. 12130, Folio 195, et seq., one of the land records of the District of Columbia and at the request of the party secured thereby, the undersigned trustee will offer for sale by public auction in front of the premises on Monday, June 7, 1965, AT TWO O'CLOCK P.M., the following described property in the District of Columbia, to wit: Lot 625 in Square 2611 in the subdivision made by Edgar D. Turner, trustee, as per plat recorded in the office of the Surveyor for the District of Columbia, in Liber 107 at Folio 80, subject to a perpetual right of way over the rear 4 feet of said lot for purposes of ingress and egress.
TERMS OF SALE: *Property will be sold subject to the balance of a prior building association deed of trust for approximately $8666.04, further particulars of which will be announced at time of sale: the purchase price above said trust to be paid in cash. A cash deposit of $750 required of purchaser at sale. . . .*

Earl M. Lapin
Eugene P. Alexander

Grant and Theresa Taylor did not see it. Sometime in the night, a few days after their confrontation with Earl Lapin, they gathered up their six children and fled Washington.

"It was late and pouring rain," Theresa recalls. "Some of

the kids was asleep because I remember carrying the smallest one out in my arms, and we was puttin things in the car, and Mama was with me then, helping put things in the car. Some of the kids was cryin and askin questions, like why we was leavin home, questions you couldn't answer, you know."

Taylor had tried to buy another house, but when the real-estate agent learned he had just lost the one he had owned for eight years for nonpayment, the answer was no. Taylor didn't even try to rent one; he was sure the answer would be the same. Word of his circumstances had reached the local credit bureau, and to the man who needed it most no one would any longer give credit. So they rented a small U-Haul trailer and filled it with as much furniture and clothes as they could. Their beds and other large pieces of furniture they abandoned. On some undetermined night in the hour of Washington's deserted streets, they drove down 14th Street, past the Washington Monument, to Route 1, heading south toward North Carolina where both Grant and Theresa Taylor had once come from.

And the heavens opened and poured down on Grant Taylor, Baptist, respectable citizen, believer in justice, hard work, God, the courts, lawyers, dignity, pride. What are we doing out in the middle of the night? Why are the kids crying? Why are we crowded in this car with everything we own hitched up behind? Heading for nowhere? Sometimes Grant Taylor thought he was going crazy.

*

Just across the Virginia state line near the town of Rocky Mount, North Carolina, in the rain, the car broke down and would go no farther. Finally some boys came along and towed the car into a yard near a gasoline station, and the Taylors abandoned the car also. It was not worth fixing up with the little money they had. They hired a man to drive them, trailer in tow, on down to Warsaw, North Carolina, where Taylor's step-grandmother lived. It was early afternoon when they arrived, and she was surprised to see them. Taylor's pride prevented him from telling her the nature of their trouble, and he was grateful she "never did ask too many questions."

Now came the most difficult trial of all, breaking up the family. In those late nights of desperation they had talked and decided that Taylor would go back to his job in Washington and the kids would have to be put out "one here, one there," so Theresa could join him later. His job was the only shred of a future they had left. Theresa for the moment moved into an empty house across the street from Taylor's grandmother and borrowed some bedding from neighbors. Taylor in a few days, full of hate for everyone, particularly Jews, took a bus back to Washington and got a furnished room at the Dunbar Hotel at 15th and U.

*

On June 7, a Monday, an auction was held in the front yard of 313 Wade Street, N.W. It was not much of a sale. The sole bidder was a William Barnett, acting on behalf of Empire Realty Services, Inc., wholly owned by Earl M. Lapin. Lapin—once holder of the note, trustee on the mortgage, forecloser on the note, and now owner of the property he had been entrusted with holding for the Taylors—paid the auctioneer the usual twenty-five dollar fee and had the deed transferred to his name. Lapin bought the Taylors' property for $2700 subject to his paying off their first mortgage of $8666 (which he had arranged) to Montgomery Federal Savings and Loan. The total sale price was $11,366, more than $2000 less than the Taylors had paid for it seven years earlier. It was, however, no more than a paper transaction; Lapin was never to put out any actual money for it. Money passed hands only when he resold it four months later for $17,000.

After about three months Theresa had found temporary homes for the children; it took much longer than she had anticipated. Theresa left their three oldest boys, Luther, ten; Wendell, nine; and Christopher, seven, with Taylor's grandmother in her big house where she also cared for foster children. Getting clearance from officials for the three Taylor boys to be added with payments for their keep to be made by Taylor, took time. Charlene, six, and Grant, Jr., five, were taken to a cousin's house farther south, far enough away so they saw their brothers and sisters only occasionally. Theresa, with her three-year-old daughter, Lelia, who, she felt, was too young to leave, then boarded the bus for Washington to join her husband in his furnished room at the Dunbar Hotel.

> "The children were heartbroken. In their own way I think they was worse off than we were. Even as small as Lelia was, she remembers. They remember the house and still say that's *their* house. They used to ask when was they going back there, would they ever get back there. They

made a lot of friends there. It was the only home they knew. Some were in school there. It was really to just tear them to pieces to pull them up and bring them here, to live with people they had never seen before they come down here. Overnight. Some of them lost weight and wouldn't eat, being away from us because we never been separated up until then.

"Little Charlene and the two little boys was writing me when I went back. Wanted to know: where is the other ones? how is they doing? when was we all going to get back together again? when was they going to see their mother? when was she coming home? and when she come home was she going to take me back? You know—just questions you couldn't answer."

•

There were nearly two years of living in furnished rooms—first in Washington and then in Fayetteville, North Carolina, where the Taylors eventually moved—before in the summer of 1967 they were able to rent a house and bring the children home. By that time the Monarch Construction Corporation was out of business and its former president, Nathan H. Cohen, who since meeting the Taylors in the summer of 1963 had signed up some 1000 other Washingtonians for a towne house front, was back in Baltimore, trying to keep one step ahead of the law.

NATHAN COHEN has claimed he did not start out dishonest. Clark says he did not know what was going on for more than a year. Salesman Daniel C. Pope, who remained with the company throughout its lifetime, told investigators everyone was so carried away by enthusiasm that they didn't realize the harm they were doing. It is true that the offices in the early days of Monarch were described as a circus—with salesmen dashing in and out, the telephone girls chattering day and night, Cohen busy on the phone with some deal, Clark holding forth with salesmen and inviting them to lunch on Monarch's expense account—but it would be a mistake to think of these two men as bumblers. They were shrewd and intelligent; they thought big, spent big, worked hard, often with meticulous attention to detail.

Monarch from the first appears well planned; the pattern of deceit consistently used by Cohen is clearly evident in the case of the Taylors, probably their first customer. The deception, essentially, was calculated to work at two levels: one in the initial selling in charge of Clark, the other in customer financing handled by Cohen. Both did their jobs well—at least in the beginning. And it is not difficult to imagine them in the summer of 1963 congratulating each other on a golden start, perhaps with accountant Stanley Silver looking on in dismay. For it appears that only he realized they were headed for disaster.

Silver later told investigators he early became troubled over his association with Monarch. He feared that Cohen's and Clark's personal extravagances, plus the vast overhead of the sales organization, would quickly consume whatever profits there were and drain the capital. For one thing, Clark insisted on a towering progression of commissions. Boiler-room girls got a percentage on telephone leads that worked out, as did canvassers. Some salesmen got a flat $300 per sale plus a certain percentage over $1500. Others shared in the profits, receiving 50 per cent of the net profits, or about $875 on a $3500 contract; the six sales managers also got a cut. Surprisingly, if the records are accurate, Cohen and Clark took out little; each drew a salary of from $250 to $300 a week through most of Monarch's lifetime. Clark also got commissions on jobs he sold personally, of which he says there were about two hundred.

Silver was also concerned that Nathan was pricing some of the jobs without knowledge of their true cost, and that Monarch was engaging in some illegal practices. Silver, a slightly built man with an earnest Glenn Ford look about him, has said that three months after Monarch began business, he tried to "part company" with his brother-in-law Cohen, mainly. because of his concern over the company's dubious practices, growing debts, and his possible personal liability as an officer. Indeed, in October 1963 Silver did resign as Monarch's treasurer, a post then assumed by Mrs. Thelma Cohen, but he did remain as accountant.

Undoubtedly, as Monarch's young president perceived it, the company's future rested on some rather complicated financial manipulations, and there must have been some suspenseful moments in the summer of 1963 when he wondered if he could organize the forces necessary to pull it off. But, little by little, with the unwitting help of some of Baltimore-Washington's respected individuals and institutions, everything fell into place.

At the heart of Monarch's operation was the promissory note ("a written promise to pay or repay a specified sum of money at a stated time or on demand") with its awesome legal implications for enforcement. As is usual in businesses of this type, it was Cohen's intention after contracts were signed to induce homeowners to sign promissory notes backed up by mortgages. These he would then sell to a financial institution at a discount, which would collect the note directly from the customer in monthly payments. However, by necessity there would be a time-lag between obtaining the contracts, finishing the work, and getting the notes signed and sold. In the meantime he had enormous bills: salesmen's commissions and salaries, construction materials and labor, office expenses. With no backlog of earnings there was scant money for a struggling new company to survive on. And it was readily apparent that without additional operating capital Monarch would be quickly defunct.

To keep Monarch afloat Cohen turned to a Baltimore businessman, Jack Arnold Gordon. Gordon at the time was a friend of Stanley Silver. Silver had been Gordon's accountant for twenty years and was a man Gordon trusted. Gordon later was to call Cohen a thief, but in July 1963, at Silver's invitation, Gordon visited the Monarch offices and soon after decided that Monarch was a "lucrative and fairly safe" investment. The agreement was made to set up a new company called the Richard Company to extend a line of credit to Monarch. Gordon put up $10,000 initially, as did his brother Bernard Gordon; Ira and N. Stanley Rosenwog, brother-owners of the Abco Lumber Company in Baltimore, put up $20,000 together; Cohen and Silver each contributed $5000. Under the arrangement, after Cohen obtained a commitment from a bank to finance a towne house front, the Richard Company would advance 75 per cent of the face value of the contract to Monarch. When the bank actually bought the note and paid Cohen, he was to repay the Richard Company with 36 per cent interest. It was interim financing and it was expensive, but it kept Monarch in business. The original limit on credit was to be $50,000. But when Monarch's business increased, the extension of credit rose to $125,000, much of it Jack Gordon's money.

Most vital to Monarch's operation was customer financing, and here too Cohen was successful. With aid from his close business associate Earl Lapin, he managed to forge connections with some of the area's most reputable savings and loan associations and even succeeded in drawing unto his enterprise the immense prestige and backing of the Federal Housing Administration (FHA). Use of the FHA's name was extremely valuable; used in advertising, it boosted the company's prestige and strengthened an association in customer's minds between Monarch and the government.

Title I of the National Housing Act—under which FHA-insured loans are granted—was adopted during the Depression to stimulate lenders to make unsecured loans to homeowners for property improvements and is dedicated to "a decent, safe, and sanitary home for everyone . . . contributing to the development and redevelopment of communities and to the advancement of the growth, wealth, and security of the Nation." The FHA does not make loans, nor does it specifically approve dealers such as Monarch. The FHA approves lending institutions which in turn approve dealer-contractors. The FHA simply *insures* the approved lenders against losses, should debtors to whom they have made "eligible" loans for property improvements fail to pay. In keeping with the law's intent, no loans can be made for frills, but only for items that "substantially protect or improve the basic livability or utility of a property." That definition would seem to make a "towne house front" façade of doubtful eligibility. Nevertheless, the decision is left up to lending institutions, although FHA officials have the power to overrule the decision. In Monarch's case they didn't.

On July 22, 1963, Monarch applied for an FHA dealership to Citizens Building and Loan Association, a firm in Silver Spring not far from Monarch's offices. And that is how Nathan Cohen came to meet Raymond Ellwood Wilson, a man he was to have lunch with nearly every week for the next two years. R. Ellwood Wilson, as he signed his name, had, since April 1962, been manager of Citizens FHA home-improvement financing department. An athletic man, then in his late thirties, Wilson was a man susceptible to Cohen's ambitions. He had, as he confessed later to Washington attorneys, a drinking problem at the time. Cohen claimed to dominate Wilson, saying he managed to process so many Monarch loans through Citizens because "I had Ellwood wrapped around my little finger." Cohen courted him, for as the person in charge of "securing and approving FHA loans, disbursing the loans and collecting them," Wilson was vital to Monarch's success.

Routinely, the Monarch FHA-guaranteed loans at Citizens passed through Ellwood Wilson, and when the time came to collect them, he as much as any other person witnessed the human misery Monarch caused. Wilson, as Citizens' collection agent, was a prime recipient of the pleading phone calls and letters and visits of desperation made after lengthy trips by bus to Silver Spring. If it affected him, he was not to admit it. Years later he said he still thought Citizens was entitled to collect on the notes.

It was Wilson who was sent to investigate Monarch's application. He later said he was not impressed by his first visit to Monarch and recommended that the company be rejected as an FHA dealer because it "was too young and moving too fast." There was also at the time another problem. Monarch's top sales executive, Myrvin C. Clark, was on the FHA's blacklist, officially called the precautionary measures list, because of his 1956 conviction for home-improvement fraud. No lending institution, forewarned, could do business with such a person without jeopardizing its standing with FHA.

Aware of this, Clark's friends had begun to put pressure,

through a series of letters, on the FHA director, then C. Edward Childs, Jr., to have Clark's name removed from the list. Clark's attorney friend John Croghan wrote a letter on his Stassen, Kephart, Sarkis and Scullin letterhead, defending Clark as a "victim of guilt by association," asserting that if Clark had had the money to appeal his conviction, he, Croghan, was certain it would have been overturned. Saul McGrane, Monarch's founding attorney, saying he had known Clark for two years, vouched for his "integrity and truly honest character," a man who need but hear "the turn of the key in the jailhouse door" to set him honest forever. Cohen also wrote a letter on his legal stationery, saying he had been "proud to have Clark for a friend for two years," which was untrue, since they had recently met. There was also a long letter of recommendation from Senator Herman Talmadge, of Clark's home state of Georgia. There may have been other pressures from influential persons, since Clark prided himself on his "Washington connections."

In any event the pressures were persuasive enough to cause FHA Director Childs to rescind the government's admonitions about Myrvin Clark. On August 2, 1963, Childs sent notice to all FHA lenders that Clark's name was henceforth removed from the precautionary measures list.

On August 15 the board of directors of Citizens Building and Loan Association approved Monarch as an FHA dealer-contractor. FHA regulations insist on a thorough investigation of a dealer to assure the lender the dealer is: 1. reliable; 2. financially responsible; 3. qualified to perform the work satisfactorily; 4. equipped to extend proper service to the customer.

"The FHA commissioner will not permit lending institutions to use insurance coverage afforded under the program for testing the dependability of dealer-contractors. The lender should have full knowledge of the principals of the firm, the salesmen, and their operation. . . ."

It cannot be said that Citizens carried out these instructions with zeal. Citizens' files show that it received a Stone's credit report on Monarch, which explicitly stated the officers had no experience in home improvements. Citizens' president C. Edwin Kline, later compelled to defend the approval of Monarch on such scanty information, said Cohen had come highly recommended to him as a "fine man" by a mutual friend in Baltimore; Kline also said he was impressed by Cohen's enthusiasm about helping the poor people of Washington.

Wilson contends that Monarch's approval was more a product of Kline's enthusiasm for more business. Citizens, Wilson says, was "anxious" for FHA business because they could get a higher interest rate—8½ per cent—than the 5 per cent they were getting on their first-mortgage loans. According to recent testimony by Wilson, when he went to Citizens they had less than a million dollars' worth of FHA on their books. By 1965, he says, Citizens had quadrupled their FHA business to $4 million. About $400,000 of it came from the Monarch Construction Corporation.

*

"That Citizens sure is a crooked bank. First time I heard of Citizens when they sent them coupons in the mail. We supposed to pay $72 a month. Citizens bank was

> already in on it, I guess. Anyway, they all in cohoots together, because otherwise they wouldn't have took that contract without hearing from us. I would just like to put up a billboard: Stay away from Citizens. When I see Citizens bank I spit. That's what they did, they robbed us of $5000 with a pencil and paper, and the government let them get away with it. That's why my lawyer said, how in the hell did this go through FHA. I guess Federal Housing is crooked too."

From September 1963 until May 1965, Citizens financed through FHA-insured loans more than 100 towne house fronts for Washington's poorer residents. Nearly every contract—"not uncoincidentally," say Washington lawyers—was for the *maximum* amount permitted by FHA under Title I, which at that time was $3500 plus interest of 8½ per cent. The final price to customers almost always ran precisely $4337.42.

According to John R. Sweeney, an investigator for the FHA, in the beginning Union Trust and American Security and Trust, banks in D. C., also bought FHA-insured paper from Monarch, "but when they discovered what was going on, they got out. Citizens didn't."

Later, when Monarch turned sour, the blame for Citizens' involvement seemed to be put on one man: R. Ellwood Wilson. But in all cases Monarch-procured loans had to be approved by an officer of the bank, which was often Kline. And there are hand-written notes extant to indicate that Kline took an active interest in Monarch, sometimes overruling Wilson's refusal of a loan. C. Edwin Kline was one of the few people retaining a friendly relationship with Monarch's officers after their activities were known.

Once a week about noon, Cohen—in later days accompanied by Marvin Greenfield, a man who had become a partner in Monarch—dropped by Citizens to deliver about half a dozen promissory notes, supported by the necessary contracts, mortgages, and completion certificates. Cohen and Wilson then went to lunch while a secretary "processed" the papers—which, as it turned out, was something more than the FHA had in mind—and made out checks to Monarch, each usually for the maximum $3500. After lunch Cohen picked up the checks and usually did not return until the following week, although he talked often to Wilson on the phone in the interim.

Although both Monarch in its advertising and the FHA insisted that an FHA loan did not require putting up property for security, Citizens consistently demanded a second mortgage, as far as can be ascertained, on all the loans made through Monarch. The reason is obvious: to make foreclosure easy. And it was a power that C. Edwin Kline, president of Citizens, and Earl Morris, vice president, the two trustees on the mortgages, did not refuse to use.

*

Since most persons, even the unsophisticated, may resist placing deeds to their homes in the custody of unknowns, especially for relatively small amounts of money and value, it was essential for Monarch often to conceal from homeowners what they were signing. A giveaway to the importance of a document is a notary public. And it is for that very reason that before a mortgage can be recorded in D. C. it must be notarized. "Historically," Noel Thompson, a lawyer handling several Monarch cases, points out, "the purpose of having deeds notarized was to prevent fraud by taking people before a neutral person, an officer of the court, or a notary public, to have them swear they were giving their deeds to somebody; this prevented deeds from being granted by inadvertence or other means. That is why the notary public and the whole ceremony of a person raising his hand and swearing he knows he is giving an interest in his property is so vital."

This, too, was an obstacle Cohen soon overcame. He had found notaries public, among them John Shughrue, then head teller at Union Trust Company where Monarch had an account, who, contrary to legal demands, would affix their seals to documents without having them signed in their presence. Shughrue had come to know Cohen after calling him at Monarch about some checks that had bounced. Thereafter Cohen began bringing the signed mortgages, several at a time, to Shughrue at the bank. In return for his seal, Cohen paid him a notary fee of fifty cents per document and gave him fifty dollars at Christmastime. Most of the mortgages that went to Citizens were notarized by Shughrue.

On another aspect of the financing, Earl M. Lapin had matters well in hand. Lapin found financial institutions that were willing to refinance for Monarch customers by giving them large new first mortgages. A new first mortgage was vital to Monarch's plans, for most of their customers were heavily in debt with, in addition to a first mortgage on their home (usually incurred at the time of purchase), a second and sometimes a third and fourth mortgage. These encumbrances usually prevented them from buying a towne house front, for no lending institution could prudently accept much less than a second mortgage. In case of default, the mortgages are paid off in numerical order—first, then second, and so on. A mortgage low down the line was apt to turn into a loss, for a house would not be worth enough to cover the debts. Furthermore, a person whose income was depleted through payments monthly on several mortgages would not be an acceptable credit risk to most financial institutions.

Through the years, however, a Monarch customer had usually paid off enough of his original first mortgage so that his own bank or another might refinance, granting him a new larger twenty-year first mortgage with a relatively low payment, probably less than he was paying cumulatively if he had other mortgages. In so doing, his other mortgages would be consolidated—paid off, leaving him with one monthly payment. Or so Lapin and Cohen represented. However, from their standpoint, the actual purpose of negotiating the new first mortgages was to sweep away the old debts, clearing the way for Monarch to obtain new loans, usually a second mortgage, for a towne house front. Since a new first mortgage rarely encompasses the total worth of a property, a second mortgage is considered a safe investment and would be accepted by a place like Citizens. Not realizing Cohen's and Lapin's intent, many assented to a new first mortgage for what they believed to be a lower monthly payment, to discover later, like the Taylors, that their debts had multiplied. The new first mortgages became a vehicle for gouging.

It was Earl Lapin, acting in the capacity of a real-estate broker, who procured the new first mortgages for Monarch customers. He obtained them from several places—Montgomery Federal Savings and Loan, Lincoln Federal Savings and Loan, Eastern Federal Savings and Loan—but most of his business was with Jefferson Federal Savings and Loan Association, an old reputable firm in the District, where he "knew someone," according to Cohen. Lapin later said he placed about three hundred new first mortgages for Monarch, about two-thirds of them at Jefferson Federal. For his services he charged homeowners a fee of usually more than $300 or $400, sometimes as much as $500. These commissions brought him more than $40,000 a year.

The settlement conference is so arcane that lawyers often call in more experienced lawyers as consultants to attend settlement conferences as protection for clients. It was here at "settlement" that Earl Lapin directed the financial manipulations that enriched himself and left those who trusted him bewildered and desperately in debt. Legally Lapin's duties lay with the homeowner; he technically represented them; they paid for his services, such as they were, and had to provide written authorization for him to act on their behalf with the bank. He had a "fiduciary responsibility" to be sure his clients understood the nature of the transaction and how their money from the new first mortgage was spent.

The procedure was thus: Lapin applied to the bank for a new first mortgage; if, after a property appraisal and credit check, the bank approved the loan, it then went through a title company. A title company guarantees, among other things, that the title the bank will hold is clear. It is also up to a title company to see that the proceeds of the new first mortgage are properly disbursed, that all old debts, taxes, fees, and so forth are paid. The papers consummating the loan are then signed at the title company by the homeowner at what is called the "settlement conference."

Under Lapin's care, homeowners were hustled off to settlement at the District Realty Title Insurance Corporation where a man named J.A. "Al" Rushing was a settlement officer, the person who sees that the funds are properly distributed. When the homeowner came to settlement, how his money was to be disbursed was already an accomplished fact, worked out by Lapin in consultation with Cohen. All the Monarch customer had to do was sign the necessary papers. "Lord, no, I didn't know what I was signing" was a common complaint.

> They're not going to ask many questions, no, they're not. Here you have very poor people, and they're ushered into a nice-looking office, and they're given to understand the man is very busy, and he's had a lot of work to do

today, and "Now we've got all this figured out and all you have to do is sign it." And they go ahead and sign it.

—Jason Souder, postal inspector
who investigated Monarch

A SETTLEMENT SHEET

Loan: Jefferson Federal S & L Assn		9000
Fire & Ext'd Coverage Ins.	35.00	
Appraisal Fee		
Commission		
Conveyancing paid		
First Deed of Trust: Liberty S & L Assn	4589.81	
Interest accrued: to May 29	34.34	
Bonus—Release charge:	12.50	
Trustee fee		
Second Deed of Trust: Auerbach & Co.	1921.47	
Interest accrued from: 4/19/64	8.60	
Trustee fee: On release	10.00	
Deferred payments subject to:		
Taxes paid thru: 7/1/64		
Taxes accrued		
Front foot benefit fr.		
Town taxes		
Special assessments		
Rent paid to		
Adjustment of interest through May:	47.13	
Deed of Trust and Note	15.00	
Appraisal fee	15.00	
Eight months' taxes toward 1965 taxes	84.00	

Commission to Empire Realty Services	450.00	
To Monarch Construction Co. for improvements	3300.00	
Title Insurance: Record Title	64.00	
Full Coverage	22.50	
Tax Report & Tax Service	2.50	
Preparing Deed: Release	10.00	
Recording Deed	12.00	
Noting and examining conveyances: trust release	6.00	
Notary fee & Notary service	4.00	
Settlement fee	24.00	
Registering Notes	5.00	
Balance due to settle		1672.85
	10,672.85	10,672.85

The settlement sheet shows how the funds of the new loan are distributed. Paying off the old mortgages (first and second deeds of trust), taxes, insurance, and a number of other items are standard, most required by law. But the settlement sheets worked out by Lapin, after those items are accounted for, bear two significant demands: a fee for Empire Realty Services—that is, Earl Lapin—and sometimes money for the Monarch Construction Corporation.

Lapin had instructions from Cohen to obtain the largest first mortgage the bank would allow, a sum that is set by bank appraisers after inspecting the property. If the sum was high enough, after all the necessary fees and mortgages were paid out, there might also be some money left over which Monarch could obtain at the time of settlement in partial or full payment for a towne house front, presumably by showing a contract substantiating the amount to the settlement officer. It was a quick way of extracting money, if there was any to extract.

So inflated was the price of the front, however, that Cohen was rarely satisfied with the amounts of money coming to him from the new first mortgages, even though in some cases it was thousands of dollars. At other times it was only a few hundred, sometimes nothing. Whatever it was, Monarch usually took it, and additionally, sometimes at the time of settlement, had the homeowner sign another new note and second mortgage, payable to Monarch for several thousand dollars for "the balance." That is apparently what happened to the Taylors, unknown to them. The new notes and second mortgages obtained at settlements Cohen then peddled to other financial institutions (such as Citizens) or individual investors.

This was the ordinary pattern, although it had variations. Sometimes a customer refused to take a new first mortgage or was denied one. Also, in some instances, Cohen was unable to sell the lesser mortgage notes—perhaps because of a customer's poor credit rating—and had to keep them for Monarch to collect on directly from customers.

The betrayal inherent in the first-mortgage manipulations was central to Monarch's operation. For without promises of a single, low monthly payment, most customers would not have signed contracts with Monarch. Yet Cohen knew as he made the promise that it was false. Many persons did not understand what they were signing at settlement and that some of their money was going to Lapin or Monarch. Some emerged confident they had consolidated and reduced their monthly payments, only to discover later that they had multiplied their debts and doubled or tripled their monthly obligations. So hazy were Lapin's explanations that a few persons emerged from negotiating a new first mortgage not even knowing they had done it.

AS MONARCH'S SALESMEN moved through Washington's near northwest, northeast, and southeast, they looked for a special clientele. Clark has said that 99 per cent of those signed up by Monarch were black. Many, as the early records reveal, were also elderly, on fixed incomes and especially susceptible to promises of a lower monthly house payment. Some could not read or write. From the beginning those Monarch sought and found were vulnerable people, poor, already in debt, frightened of losing their homes, people in helpless situations who could be taken advantage of.

The customer roster grew: *Miles and Sara Townsend, Willie Thomas, Mattie Younger, Neamon and Annie Perry, Mary Hughes, Pearl Wright, Lillian Jefferson, Jesse and Martha Ellis, Augustus and Susie Rice, Arthur and Elease Nelson, Homer Roberson, William and Dorothy Holmes, Harriet Crannell, Lucille Johnson, Judson Terry. . . .*

And so did evidence of the misleading sales pitches.

Monarch's salesmen used some initiative in improvising sales pitches but in general followed a similar pattern. They stressed that the towne house fronts would double or triple the value of the homes and save them from urban renewal; they showed photos of demolished homes and newspaper clippings of D. C.'s urban renewal activities; they often took prospective customers for rides to view completed fronts. They posed as urban renewal officials, housing inspectors, other government agents, usually by innuendo. They stated that all jobs had to be approved by an advisory committee of civic leaders, including Roy Wilkins of the National Association for the Advancement of Colored People, who had no connection with Monarch.

> "When they come in they was *so* sweet, and they just talk, talk. And all they was talkin about was Mr. Roy Wilkins. Mr. Wilkins gonna do this and Mr. Wilkins gonna do that. Mr. Wilkins was puttin on this program and seeing all these people. They showed us a lot of photos, but I don't know who they were, cause there were a lot of white people and black people, and Mr. George, he said all the people was in with them in the program. They didn't call anybody's name but Mr. Roy Wilkins; he said that he was having a meeting down in Lincoln Park. Oh, why don't ya all come down to the meetin sometime. And he say the program is for the colored people, to help the colored people improve their property. That the way Mr. George splained it to us. He said he was gonna take the note back to Mr. Wilkins and see if Mr. Wilkins would approve it."

Scipio Darden, Gladys Garley, Tyrone and Gladys Smith, Juanita Lamb, Julius and Ruby Barrett, Varis and Hattie Bailey, Bertha Hayes, Hughie Lee Ledbetter, Clara Marlow, Waymond and Pauline Powell . . .

> "Yes, ma'am, I'm sorry I ever met them. They cheated me, and they didn't half do the work. My back porch upstairs is a mess, and I mean I'm tellin you the truth, I *work* for my money, and I try to do the right thing and pay my bills and be a Christian. But you know what they

did. They give me *one* contract and they didn't get me the material that they had on the first contract. And the man come down here, his name was—he's a little young fellow cause he hadn't been married too long—*Pope*, that's *him*. Daniel Pope come here, and Mr. Pope stole that contract. I said stole, for we was lookin at them and he had another contract, and you know he took that old contract with him and put another one in the envelope for me. The first one was for a lot less money, cause I had counted up, and I said, "Well, I can get by, I can do this real good." But that *other* one! Oh, my golly, it was terrible. To tell the truth, I *never* wish people bad luck, but I said to myself I'm gonna pray for him, and like God say, what you sow you reap."

The towne house front was advertised for $1500, but only a few sold for that, usually as "showplaces." According to Clark, the standard price went steadily upward—to $2200, then $2700, $3500, and by the end of 1964 "the sky was the limit." However, these standard prices issued to salesmen are unreliable, for it was part of Cohen's pricing system to rewrite the contracts, "bumping up the price," as he called it. He or another Monarch representative would, on some pretext, retrieve the original contract and substitute a higher-priced one (or sometimes two or three contracts which split the cost of the job). In fact, many towne house fronts eventually cost $6000 and $7000, and there are existing contracts for $9900.

The materials were cheap, the workmanship often shoddy, and that the front was overpriced is shown by Monarch's records. In the beginning the company employed workmen to erect the fronts under the supervision of Thomas Proutt, construction manager. The cost to Monarch for a standard two-story towne house front in October 1963, according to Proutt, was $600 in materials and $300 in labor and trucking, a total of $900. Later, in February 1964, when Silver's fears were realized and Monarch was in financial difficulty, Cohen set up a subsidiary, Towne House Construction Corporation, which he hoped could obtain credit being denied to Monarch. With Proutt in charge and Thelma Cohen as director and secretary, Towne House handled all construction, making Monarch strictly a sales organization. Towne House then took out its own profit and overhead and billed Cohen—that is, Monarch—for the jobs. The charge to Monarch for a towne house front then jumped to about $2000, which worried Cohen none, for he was destined, he thought, to make profits from both sources.

Thomas Covington, Royale and Janice Prince, Julius and Johnnie Mae Roberson, Hilliard Mitchell, Lottie Fleming, Lucius and Maude Dunbar, Shirley Smith, Cleotis Moore, Hosea and Ella Williams, John Patterson, Marie Spencer . . .

Some persons were deceived into buying a towne house front when they only wanted interior repairs. Not surprisingly (as Clark, who in his other home-improvement ventures had visited many a poor man's home, must have known), persons living in "a deteriorating neighborhood in danger of slipping into a slum condition" had more pressing needs for home improvements than an aluminum towne house front façade. Inside, stairways were rotting, plaster was cracked, plumbing was inoperable, porches and other structural supports were collapsing, kitchens were in disrepair. Some of the houses Monarch salesmen visited had been cited for housing violations.

However, Cohen's profits, he believed, depended on the mass-produced front, quick and easy to install. Interior repairs were tedious and custom-tailored, requiring highly paid tradesmen and yielding small profit. Consequently, Monarch salesmen were instructed to discourage interior improvements, and Monarch disguised its intent through rhetoric: Phase I and Phase II of the urban renewal program. Phase I, the towne house front, customers were told, was a prerequisite to Phase II, interior repairs. However, after the front was erected, many discovered that Phase II was a fiction. Most of the loan a customer was able to get was drained off for the front. If there was sufficient money left to guarantee a substantial profit to Cohen, he would write a completely new contract for the interior work (which homeowners had been led to believe was included in the original price) and subcontract the job to a local home-improvement firm which rarely completed it to the homeowner's satisfaction. If there was no money available, he simply wrote the interior repairs out of the original contract, as he apparently did with the Taylors.

By mid-September, after two months in business, Monarch had sold fifty-five towne house fronts. Clark called a sales meeting to set large new quotas for the following month, and

Cohen threw a party for the Monarch staff at Washington's International Inn.

*

Complaints about Monarch came early—within the second month of operation—and apparently Cohen handled them with finesse. It is said that once when he learned a salesman had misrepresented himself to a policeman's wife, he himself, anticipating a complaint, reported the incident to the Department of Licenses, charging that an unknown salesman was using Monarch's name, discrediting a "reputable firm." Julian Green, granter of licenses, later praised Monarch's prompt attention to complaints: "When informed of a complaint, Cohen was down here the next morning. We got better cooperation from him in handling complaints than any other home-improvement contractor."

But because Monarch was launched on a grand scale—with mass mailings, intensive telephone solicitation, and expensive brochures—it could not escape the notice of other businessmen and government agencies. In January 1964 the D. C. home-improvement licenses came up for renewal, accompanied by the first serious grumblings from the community about Monarch. John H. Haas, a contractor and vice president of the General Improvement Contractors Association, had seen Monarch's promotional brochures, which he said were "saturating the Capitol Hill area," and objected strenuously. Experienced in inner-city property restoration, Haas was incensed by Monarch's claims that a towne house front constituted a "complete renovation" which would "triple the value of your home." "Monarch pretended to rehabilitate," he recalled recently, "and what they actually did was to put up a cosmetic front, and rehabilitation has nothing to do with cosmetics. Rehabilitation means a thorough and serious structural, mechanical restoration of property. They did not touch the heating system, the plumbing system, the wiring, the condition of the walls, ceilings or floors; they didn't even look at the back side of the house. Every time they mentioned they were 'restoring,' I got redder and redder in the face."

Haas, convinced that Monarch's total operation was a fraud, protested to the Department of Licenses and Inspections, the U.S. Attorney's office in the District, the Federal Housing Administration (FHA), and the Federal Trade Commission. Haas urged Green of the Department of Licenses to refuse to renew Monarch's home-improvement license for 1964, as well as Myrvin Clark's salesman's license. Haas, although he didn't know it, was joined in his plea by the D. C. Police Department, which reaffirmed its disapproval of a renewed salesman's license for Clark, and this time also recommended disapproval of a contractor's license for Monarch, mainly because of the bad credit rating of Thomas Proutt, now a vice president of the company.

Julian Green's notation at the bottom of the police report reads: "Met with Clark on 2/6/64. No change in circumstances since approval of license in 1963, except that he has been reinstated as an approved FHA dealer. No justification for denial of 1964 license." Both Clark and Monarch were given licenses to operate for another year.

BY THIS TIME—early 1964—some of the destructive impact of Monarch, which was to worsen, was becoming apparent. Many families in what each thought was isolation were undergoing their private terrors attributable to Monarch. The company, on the other hand, was in decay. The initial boost given Monarch by the Cohen family's investment, as well as by the Richard Company, had worn off. Although sales had been respectable, the company was in the red. According to a financial statement dated December 19, 1963, Monarch in its first five months had sold $324,319 worth of towne house fronts and other home improvements. However, when the cost of the jobs ($202,525), selling expenses ($87,285), and general and administrative expenses ($47,930) were deducted, there was a net loss of $13,421. Cohen was later to blame Clark, claiming he had "run through $150,000 of Monarch's money" in the first six months.

Cohen was now desperate for money and besieged by creditors on all sides. Only the bills necessary to keep operating, such as for telephones, were being paid. Creditors were suing. Even Paul McGarvey, first Monarch president and attorney, sued for back attorney's fees of $300. In early 1964 Monarch owed the federal government $5000 for delinquent income taxes. In June 1964 the State of Maryland got a lien against Cohen for $1462.30 for unemployment insurance. The state also wanted its income taxes, which supposedly had been withheld from employees' salaries. Cohen, after weeks of prodding, sent a check; it bounced.

Monarch wasn't paying its subcontractors for the interior repairs many customers demanded, and sometimes did not even pay its own subsidiary, Towne House Construction. Salesmen were quitting mainly because they were not getting their commissions, and were particularly angered that they were paid a percentage only on the original contract and not on the final price after it was "bumped up" by Cohen. By the spring of 1964 Clark's sales force had shrunk to four or five men. The old pro himself was often now on the streets as an ordinary salesman. Clark, disgusted with the operation, quit at least three times in 1964, but always came back, he said recently, "when that weekly paycheck came round." And the selling continued, though construction often did not. Nathan Cohen apparently could not let go of the prospect of fortunes from a plan that on its face looked so easy: his "American Towne House Program of Urban Renewal."

A financial statement for August 1964 shows that Monarch during the first seven months of that year sold $414,342 worth of towne house fronts and had a net loss of $97,000. There was no money throughout 1964 for supplies and labor to complete the jobs. The company was surviving only on prospects of future earnings and using current income to pay past debts. Consequently those who continued to sign up for towne house fronts were trapped in the company's insolvency and Cohen's ambitions.

Throughout Washington's poor areas one can still see the remains of towne house fronts, only partially completed, abandoned by workers at various stages of the work. A couple of workmen might come by for a few hours a day—sometimes at night—and not return for weeks, months, if at all. Monarch customers tell of having their yards filled with rubbish and rotting materials, their porches and front entrances unusable for months, doors that were removed in cold weather and not replaced.

Interiors of houses were also often torn up, abandoned by subcontractors' workmen who were never paid. The poor, in despair, called Monarch, usually to be told Mr. Cohen was not in. Sometimes the calls were referred to "our subcontractor, Mr. Proutt." Customers could not know that Monarch and Mr. Proutt, of Towne House Construction, were the same. If customers could find anyone to talk to, they were usually told it was some kind of error and workmen would be back in the morning. Customers in frustration waited weeks, even months, their houses wrecks, but no one came. Some finally hired other contractors to clean up the mess, compounding their debts.

Cohen, however, did try to complete enough of the work so he could make legal claim to his money. It was Monarch's policy at least to "spike" a job. Spiking is a term among disreputable home-improvement companies, meaning to "put in the first nail," pretend to start the work so the customer believes he can't back out of the contract. Some homeowners received no more than Monarch's routine spiking job, consisting of a few aluminum strips over the door or swatches of paint across the bottom half of the house. Monarch had one man, Chris Breierly, who even in the leanest of times drove around in a truck with, as one salesman later said, "a keg of case-hardened nails and some furring strips and paint." When a salesman obtained a contract, he was to call the office immediately so the spiker could be dispatched to the address. Salesman Daniel Pope later recalled for investigators that once Breierly arrived and tacked up some strips while he, Pope, having concluded a contract, was still at the customer's house. According to Pope, the buyer, an elderly widow, tried later to cancel the contract, but "Monarch sued her and got three hundred and thirty-five dollars from her for the furring strips."

Some persons were cruelly caught between Monarch and the subcontractors. Unable to collect their money from Cohen, some subcontractors turned on the property owner, demanding payment, although the homeowner had already indebted himself by signing papers payable to Cohen. Many customers in 1964 were being harassed by phone calls from bitter, unpaid workmen. One such customer was Monroe Summers, who, with his wife, Ella, had agreed to have the back part of their house repaired since the roof was leaking and an enclosed back porch was in such bad repair they could not get a new first mortgage to consolidate their debts as they wished. Monarch hired Better Homes Construction Company to do the remodeling.

The work they did still makes Mrs. Summers sick with disappointment: "They caused me a lot of trouble, and I never will forget it. Every time I come through here and see how they didn't fix it like they should, I think of it." The floor they installed is not level, the ceiling, which they replaced without removing the old one, has buckled, the aluminum siding on the back has deteriorated, and there are no electrical outlets in the room. Nevertheless, Ella Summers recalls, she signed papers to pay for the work under duress from "a heavy-set man" who claimed to be from her home town in North Carolina, probably Myrvin Clark, who consistently changed his Southern birthplace to conform with that of his customers.

Cohen then sold the Summers note, which was inflated to $4337.45, to Citizens Building and Loan and received his usual check for $3500 for an FHA-insured loan. Cohen, however, refused to pay the subcontractor the $1940 for labor and materials on the Summers house. Furious, the subcontractor didn't pay his own workmen, and both he and the workmen began hounding the Summerses for payment, calling during the day and night and threatening to take their home if they didn't pay. The Summerses were bewildered and distraught by the harassment. "So I kept tellin him I didn't have any money, I couldn't pay them. He said, well, he been down at the other place, and he and Monarch had had a fight, and they wouldn't pay him no money at all, and somebody had to pay him." In November the subcontractor filed for a mechanic's lien on the Summers home. Anyone who performs work on a building and remains unpaid can take out a mechanic's lien for value of the work to protect his interest. To enforce the lien he must then sue, and if he is successful, the property can be sold to satisfy the debt. In the meantime a mechanic's lien is a cloud on the title to the property and detrimental to credit ratings.

Caught in the middle and already heavily in debt through a contract with Monarch higher than she had been led to believe, Ella Summers was nearly hysterical with worry over losing the house. Her high blood pressure became critical, and she had to leave her job as a clerk in a shop, where the workmen also called her demanding money. Later she suffered a nervous breakdown, according to her attorney, and was hospitalized for weeks. In 1971 Mrs. Summers, nearly blind and unable to work, was still fearful that "those men" who harassed her would return to harm her.

The mechanic's lien was not enforced, but the Summerses did pay the full $4337.45 to Citizens; they paid $72 a month, and when Monroe Summers retired after twenty-nine years of work at a dairy, they took $1200 of his retirement money to finish off the debt.

Many of Monarch's victims did not seek help from attorneys unless threatened with loss of property, as were Monroe and Ella Summers, or when forced to defend themselves in suits instituted by Monarch or other interested parties. What immediately occurs to a middle-class person—seizing the law for self-defense—does not always occur to the poor, or if it does, they may reject it. Traditionally, the law has not been a weapon of the poor.

> *The poor man . . . has little reason to believe [the law] is his guardian; he has every reason to believe it is an instrument of the Other Society, of the well-off, the well-educated, the well-dressed, and the well-connected. The poor man is cut off from the society and the protection of its laws. . . . Seldom in his struggles with a finance company, a merchant, landlord, or a rigid official is the poor man even aware that he has rights which perhaps are being violated. If he knows, he may have no way to protect them. And finally, even if he is aware of legal services,*

he might well be deterred by irrational fear of cost, shame or further exploitation.

—Nicholas de B. Katzenbach
when he was Attorney General
of the United States.

When those who dealt with Monarch were later asked why they did not go to lawyers for help, many said they were ashamed to admit they had been duped; they believed, too, that they were alone in their "stupidity." Many did not understand until years later that they had been victimized, and some who did felt it was their own mistake; they assumed the consequences stoically as a lesson dearly learned. Some, especially the elderly, displayed a deep fear of the law or viewed going to court as a disgrace or un-Christian or immoral. To nearly all, legal advice was considered a costly expenditure with an unpredictable outcome. Neighborhood Legal Services, funded by the Office of Economic Opportunity to represent the impoverished at no charge, did not open until January 1965 in the District, as in other cities. Until that time the choice of the poor was Legal Aid, operated by the D. C. Bar Association, or private attorneys entailing fees impossible for persons already smothered by debt. One woman, confronted with paying off a note filled in by Cohen for $5000, tells of paying a $50 legal consultation fee, more than a week's earnings, to be told there was nothing to do but pay. She could ill-afford a second opinion.

Indeed persons who attempted to assert their legal rights sometimes received incompetent legal counsel which harmed more than helped them, imprisoning them in their debt through settlements and court judgments. At that time the machinations of the whole Monarch operation were still buried, the pattern of the fraud unknown. In ignorance of the facts—and in no position to undergo an extensive investigation to ascertain the facts—some attorneys informed clients they had no defense, that they were obligated to pay off the contracts and promissory notes they had supposedly signed. It is apparent also that some attorneys thought their clients were confused or lying. Stories of "missing contracts," which Cohen had retrieved and destroyed, sounded incoherent. When confronted with accusations, Cohen wrote earnest letters to attorneys, insisting that he was doing everything possible to please the client. Whom was one to believe—a fellow attorney, a respectable businessman, or an inarticulate black man who was perhaps trying to evade his debts? Some chose to believe Cohen.

Most importantly, few attorneys had the foresight or courage to attack what is called the "holder in due course" doctrine of commercial law. And this was the legal trap in which most of Monarch's customers found themselves. When Cohen sold the promissory notes at a discount to financial institutions, the financial institution as the new owner then assumed a special legal status known as a "holder in due course." Under this doctrine, the financial institution is regarded as an "innocent third party," merely a moneylender and not responsible for irregularities in the original transaction. Accordingly, the courts generally hold, the financial institution—if it bought the note "in good faith, for value and with no notice of a defect"—is entitled to collect the note, even though the signatures were obtained through misrepresentations (thus, even if Cohen lied in procuring the note) or the work was never completed or perhaps even begun.

The historical purpose of the law is to guarantee the free flow of negotiable paper vital to commercial dealings. It presupposes that the two parties making the contract are of equal sophistication and bargaining power, which is generally true of businessmen giving notes. But in consumer transactions, where persons of little education and knowledge are pitted against the likes of Nathan Cohen, the law can produce personal disasters by enforcing the collection of unjust debts. Essentially, the law in consumer matters provides a shield behind which financial institutions can hide, and "see no evil," because they refuse to look. It was on the validity of the holder-in-due-course doctrine that institutions, such as Citizens Building and Loan and others who bought notes from Cohen, relied.

Within the past ten years, particularly within the past five, the doctrine of holder in due course in consumer matters has been successfully assaulted by pioneering lawyers. Some states have even outlawed its use in consumer transactions. Still, many lawyers schooled years ago regard the law as unassailable and promissory notes as virtually unbreakable. Some unfortunate Monarch victims consulted such lawyers, whom Judge Theodore Newman of D. C. Superior Court refers to as "curbside lawyers" (unwilling to get into the fray), and who consequently, in the Judge's words, were "victimized by the conventional wisdom of the law." When shown signed documents, some attorneys advised their clients not to fight because they did not stand a chance of winning and would only be wasting money in legal costs.

Throughout Monarch's lifetime it was essential to the company's existence to obtain homeowners' legally binding signatures on the proper documents. With this accomplished, Cohen could often peddle the notes or extract monies from the new first mortgages whether or not the work was finished. Getting the signatures was Cohen's specialty, although some of it was also handled by workmen and other salesmen. Monarch customers were later to come forth with a whole repertory of the company's techniques, including intimidation with racist overtones, distraction, misrepresentations, and, it is said, if all else failed, forgery.

Many of Cohen's victims, primed by a 350-year heritage of slavery, were trusting and acquiescent. Few realized the awesome consequences of what they were signing or that they were putting deeds to their homes in Cohen's care. Some thought if what they were signing was really important they would have been taken before a notary public as they had been for previous transactions. Quite a few could not read—some not at all or not well enough to comprehend what they signed. Ashamed of their inability, some say that they did not read the documents because they didn't have their glasses or the prescription was faulty. These persons relied entirely on their faith in Mr. Cohen.

Cohen told his customers they were signing construction permits, loan applications, unbinding letters of agreement, endorsements, letters of reference, credit applications. The most powerful inducement was that the papers were "necessary to get the new loan to get their debts consolidated and the monthly payments down." Under that guise, a whole stack of papers could be signed, including some new notes and second, third, even fourth mortgages.

*

When asked why they signed:

> "I had to do what the man say. Sometimes you have to trust a man. This man says these things had to go down to the title people, this was for to get the two notes where we owed on the house consolidated. That's all he told me. I asked him. He say more loan, all this is for you to get your two notes consolidated, that's all."

> "Mother's old, she's seventy-seven now; her and I are both widows. What happened, you know, she can't write, and she had made her X one day on this paper when I wasn't here, and he just filled in her name. Then he came one day and said, 'Well, your mother signed, and you have to sign beside her,' and I did."

> "When I came in—I went downtown like when you buying a house—that same man came to my house and *made* me sign some more papers. I remember I was sittin in the hall, and I sit there and I was just a-cryin and carryin on, and he told me if I didn't sign—he say I shoot you if you don't sign this paper. I didn't see any gun or

> anything, but he said it to me. He said it was something I supposed to sign. I don't know just what it was, something he wrote it hisself."

Several persons reported they were invited to the Silver Spring offices of Monarch to discuss their grievances and then were kept there for hours, virtual prisoners, until under coercion they agreed to sign some papers.

One woman tells of Cohen rushing into her house one winter night, pretending to be cold, hungry, thirsty. Did she have some water? An apple? Oh, yes, here were the papers she was to sign, right away. He had to leave immediately to catch a plane. Several persons say that on the very night Cohen was at their house he was on his way to Miami or New York "in a terrible rush."

Since the papers were usually blank when signed, customers had only vague conceptions of what prices they were to pay. Some to their horror discovered later that Cohen had filled in their notes for $6000 and $7000, sums that had no relationship whatever to the value of the work. In fact, he often split the contracts to justify unconscionable prices, three contracts, for example, for a single towne house front: $3500 for the aluminum and the towne house door and windows; another $1000 for the shutters, another $725 for the trim.

Many of the notes Monarch took also were "balloons"—that is, a $5000 note might call for sixty monthly payments of $60 each, leaving at the end of five years a single large payment of $1400, which the customer didn't suspect and probably couldn't pay. The victim would then, when the note came due, have to refinance, guaranteeing his continued indebtedness.

Of special importance to Monarch for those notes sold to Citizens as FHA-insured loans were the completion certificates demanded by the FHA as a precaution against the premature distribution of funds. They were little protection, however, for Monarch's customers. Even those who realized what they were signing were often enticed to do so under the pretense that Monarch could not complete the work unless they got "an advance from the bank." Some completion certificates, Monarch salesmen said later, were signed at the same time as the contracts. Citizens rarely checked to see if the construction was finished before giving Cohen his money. It was a fact of banking that many, when pressured for payment, could not comprehend.

> "Why'd that bank give that man all that money without askin me? It would a only took one phone call, and I would have told them: Don't let him have it. He ain't done the work yet."

BY THE LATE SPRING of 1964, with Monarch on the verge of collapse, Nathan Cohen looked for a new investor. He asked salesman Dan Pope for ideas, and Pope told him he could think of only one man with that kind of money: Marvin Greenfield, an entrepreneur around Washington, who, among other interests, had a finance company, Universal Acceptance Corporation. Pope had once run a used-car business in D. C. and sold contracts to Greenfield.

Cohen contacted Greenfield and went to his office at 6400 Georgia Avenue sometime in the summer of 1964. As Cohen recalled later, he told Greenfield his credit had dried up with the Richard Company and he needed money. Greenfield's partner, Patrick Collins, who was present at the meeting, took an instant dislike to Cohen: "I told Marvin [in Cohen's presence], 'this guy's a thief and he's going to rob you.'" Cohen reportedly laughed.

Against Collins' advice, Greenfield lent Cohen $10,000 initially, with customers' contracts put up as security, and gradually put more money behind the company. Then the day came, Cohen recently recalled, that Greenfield told him he was dissatisfied with his position of investor and "was looking for ownership in a business." Cohen was agreeable, so Greenfield asked to see Monarch's financial statements and minutes of directors' meetings. As Stanley Silver was to recount later, the financial statements were fixed up with an "unorthodox accounting system" to look rosier, and since there never had been any directors' meetings, Cohen prepared some corporate minutes and backdated them for Greenfield. Greenfield's accountant, Vic Becker,* advised him 100 per cent against buying into Monarch, pointing out that the company had never been more than a "shell." But as Collins later said, Marvin was the kind of man who could not resist chasing a dollar. "He had this tremendous drive and urge to make money." In October Greenfield became half-owner of Monarch. On October 10 Thelma Cohen sent a letter to the Riggs Bank instructing them that she, Nathan, and now also Marvin Greenfield, "manager," could sign checks for Monarch. Mrs. Cohen, however, was no longer an investor in Monarch. Greenfield bought her out, paying her $10,000 in cash and $40,000 in a note due in six months. He also gave Silver a note for $10,000. Silver's withdrawal infuriated investor Jack Gordon, but Silver assured him he would continue to oversee the finances, guarding Gordon's interest as if it were his own.

Greenfield, a bespectacled man of medium height, was a millionaire, and he was introduced at sales meetings as the new half-owner who was going to save the company. It is difficult to determine exactly how much money Greenfield did put into the business. He has said he invested $150,000 in Monarch and lost $45,000, a sum that his lawyer says grew in Greenfield's mind as the years passed. In any event the sudden infusion of money, plus Greenfield's presence, revitalized the company. By January 1965 some forty salesmen were back on the payroll. Greenfield, like Cohen before him, suspended his interest in other projects and moved to 10111 Colesville Road, where he shared an office with Cohen. Clark later said the two were inseparable: "They lived together from morning to night." Greenfield also brought his own secretary, bookkeeper, and a number of salesmen Clark referred to as "dynamiters," the worst in the trade.

Cohen recently said of Greenfield: "He spent the first thirty days, I would say, sort of following me around and watching what I did and learning the operation of Monarch. Then he began to take over more and more of my functions and assert his presence and to make decisions until finally it culminated in his actually dominating the operation and my following him around." This is undoubtedly an exaggeration, for it is difficult to entertain an image of the proud Cohen so docile. The statement was made at a time when it was to Cohen's advantage to put as much blame as possible on Greenfield. It is undeniable, though, that Greenfield participated actively in Monarch and made changes. Under his influence, Monarch became more aggressive. According to salesmen, he instructed them to abandon any fixed price on the front and write contracts for "whatever the market would bear." Contracts, consequently, after Greenfield's entrance, show a marked price increase.

The new partner began dictating the terms of some of the new first mortgages and attending settlement conferences. Al Rushing, settlement officer at District Realty, later told investigators that Greenfield often got into arguments with homeowners who discovered their debts had not been consolidated as promised. Greenfield reportedly told them it was too late to back out and he would sue them if they didn't go through with the transaction. Rushing, who notarized most of the second mortgages generated by the settlements, admitted later he realized homeowners were being gouged and little understood what they were signing. But Rushing remained silent. He said later that Greenfield gave him a suit for Christmas.

One matter that disturbed Greenfield about the settlements was the enormous income received by Earl Lapin in brokerage fees. During 1964, when business was slow, Lapin earned $47,614 from Monarch transactions. Later he was to earn that much again in the first half of 1965. When Lapin refused to kick back part of the proceeds to Monarch, Greenfield insisted Cohen obtain a real-estate broker's license, which he did. Finally, in July 1965, Cohen and Greenfield set up their own brokerage firm, named Roseanne Realty after Cohen's wife, to handle the new first mortgages. Acting as broker for Roseanne was the expert salesman Daniel Pope. Pope was put on a 25 per cent commission with a minimum of $100 from each settlement. The rest went to Cohen and Greenfield, and Lapin was out.

Greenfield also became Cohen's partner in the nocturnal sojourns to get the contracts rewritten and jacked up. Greenfield was introduced as "Mr. Stevens" or "Mr. Anderson," as he was at settlement conferences, to hide his identity. Greenfield never officially assumed any position as officer with which investigators could later incriminate him. Greenfield was an antique collector; as Cohen was later to say, Marvin often distracted the poor with talk of antiques while Cohen got the papers signed.

> "See that piece of furniture in the dining room. He went to there. 'Oh, where did you get this from? Where? Oh, I would love to have this piece of antique.' And he went to talkin on that, you know—he had on glasses, that's all I remember about him—and then my husband say I have another piece upstairs. Oh, let's go upstairs and see that. See, that was to get his mind off of Mr. Cohen. Then they went upstairs and they stayed upstairs for a long time, and Mr. Cohen was writing all the while they was upstairs. And then they come back down and Mr. Cohen he had my husband to sign, then he called me, and he said to me, 'Press real hard, now press *real* hard or it won't go through.' I don't know what he had up under there. See, that's why they got all those papers. . . ."

*

Cohen and Greenfield, according to Myrvin Clark, went out at night after the contracts came in to "review" them with homeowners. Recently Clark told a jury of "going out in the field one evening" with Cohen and Greenfield to "review contracts." According to Clark, they went to a customer's house to review a $350 contract, where "Nate introduced Greenfield as Stevens, the man in charge of the building and loan operation. Greenfield reviewed the contract, then Nate told them they would have to take a day off and come in the office to fill out the papers. Mr. Greenfield said if they would fill them out that evening, they would save time. There were two sets, one for $3500 and one for $3400, making $6900." Cohen, said Clark, explained that with the new set of contracts they would pay only $69 a month, whereas with the old one they would pay

$72, so they would be saving $3 a month. The homeowner, who before their visit had been obligated for $3500, was now obligated to pay $6900 for exactly the same work.

Clark, who professed to be unaware, until that time, that the contracts were being regularly jacked up, then told the court that the three of them got back in the car.

"And then what happened, Mr. Clark?"

"They asked me, 'Well, what do you think?'

"I said, 'I think we're all going to jail.' "

COHEN'S FINANCIAL TROUBLES with the entry of Greenfield were now solved, but as Clark perhaps foresaw, worse difficulties were fast approaching. Marvin Greenfield, to his everlasting regret, arrived on the scene just in time to see Monarch's legal problems—which had been increasing—explode into public view and eventually into the U.S. Attorney's office. The source of the trouble was a man by the name of Leopold Julius Heinrich Herwig.

On April 23, 1964, two salesmen had reached the home of Bessie Newberry, a woman in her sixties, one of the few whites Monarch contacted. Miss Newberry at the time was a secretary to a judge, had a large house, and rented rooms. Living on the premises was an old friend and her attorney (whom she subsequently married), Leopold Julius Heinrich Herwig, known as Colonel Herwig because of his World War I commission. Herwig, then seventy-eight, a short bald man, had practiced law in Washington since 1923 and was known as an "eccentric" and a "rugged individualist" by his colleagues. He was present the night the two Monarch salesmen arrived, and Cohen said later it was a visit he wished his salesmen had never made. For the eccentric colonel was a man of enormous energy who doggedly pursued Cohen for years.

Bessie Newberry was receptive to the salesmen, Lyle Von Wagner and Robert Freed (who told Herwig he was a Mennonite), for she had dreams of converting her house into three apartments for rental income after her retirement. Von Wagner—who at that time was on the FHA's blacklist because of illicit home-improvement activities in Texas—went over the house, according to Herwig, and after about fifteen minutes came up with an estimate of $12,886. Herwig urged Miss Newberry to accept it, since it was the lowest estimate she had had. She did. As the two were about to leave, Von Wagner mentioned a towne house front, but both Newberry and Herwig said they weren't interested.

The next afternoon the two men came back on what Herwig called "a surprise visit" in his absence and induced Bessie Newberry to sign another contract for a towne house front, insisting it was necessary to procure an FHA loan. Troubled, Herwig called Monarch's president, who came to the house. Herwig recalls he was charmed by Cohen and urged Miss Newberry to "give Cohen a chance," even though she had become suspicious. A few days later workmen came to put up the towne house front, and it was apparent they hardly knew what they were doing: large sections of the front were left unpainted, the window frames were lightweight, and the old screens were put back in. Still, with Cohen's assurances the work would be finished to her satisfaction, Bessie Newberry signed a completion certificate stating the work was done. Around the same time Cohen and Clark came to her office in the courthouse and persuaded her to sign a mortgage to her house.

Earl Lapin, a stranger to both Herwig and Newberry, then called and asked them to come to a settlement conference to complete the loan. Herwig later admitted he was "somewhat unfamiliar with the situation" and confused by it. But Herwig did notice Lapin's $380 fee for procuring the loan and recalled an article in the old *Liberty* magazine, written by Franklin D. Roosevelt while campaigning for the Presidency, warning against such fees. Herwig objected to the fee, but Lapin stood firm and finally Herwig allowed Miss Newberry to sign. It was not until Herwig got home that Friday night and had time to ponder the facts over the weekend that he understood she had taken out a $9000 loan to put towne house fronts on her two garages, that none of the money went to remodeling the apartments. The nature of the enterprise began to dawn on Herwig.

Immediately Monday morning he called the District Realty Title Insurance Corporation, which had handled the negotiations, and canceled the loan. Earl Lapin was furious and called Herwig to tell him so. But the old colonel was not intimidated. By this time he realized that the original contract for the $12,000 renovations, signed by Von Wagner, had disappeared from Miss Newberry's house, "stolen by Cohen," he later charged.

Colonel Herwig that summer began making inquiries around the Capitol Hill neighborhood and found others with similar stories. By September 19, 1964, the Colonel had enough material to file suit in District Court against Nathan Cohen, the Monarch Construction Corporation, Towne House Construction Corporation, Union Trust Company (the bank that bought the FHA-guaranteed note), Earl Lapin, and Empire Realty Service, Inc., for fraud and damages of $75,000.

It was not the first such action directed at Monarch, but it was the broadest and as it turned out the most to the point:

Herwig branded Nathan Cohen's enterprise the "American Towne House Racket."

> *Defendants [Cohen, Monarch, and Towne House Construction] have been engaged in the District of Columbia since or on about to wit, April 1964, in the perpetration of its American Towne House Racket under the guise and pretext of procuring an FHA loan to finance certain home improvements and conversion into apartments of the landowner's property for the production of income. . . . Said defendants, in the matter of obtaining FHA bank loans to finance certain home improvements for payment therefor to said defendants . . . did knowingly, and willfully, at the time and place herein set forth, by trickery, schemes, devices and false pretenses, represent to said owners that it was necessary to install the American Towne House Front on their property to obtain the FHA loans and to have the building construction done. The homeowners believed and relied upon the truthfulness of said representations and, accordingly, consented to the American Towne House construction on their property. Said representations were false and untrue, contrary to the requirements of the National Housing Act, and . . . they were known to the said Defendants to be false and untrue. Nevertheless, said FHA loans were obtained and paid to said Defendants for the installation of the American Towne House Front, which was poorly, negligently and unsatisfactorily done. The home improvements and the constructions of the apartments were never done.*

On the night of September 30, Cohen, Clark, and Earl Lapin, after calling Bessie Newberry from Lapin's office, went to her house. According to Herwig, the three men forced their way into the house and attempted to frighten her into not pursuing her lawsuit. Lapin reportedly insulted her and threatened to sue her for defamation, slander, and libel for the charges she had made against him in her suit. Throughout Lapin's harangue, charged Herwig, Cohen and Clark stood by, acting as an audience for Lapin, "subjecting Miss Newberry to ridicule and scorn and contempt by their acts of silly giggling and derisive laughter."

Colonel Herwig was deeply offended. "I think any man who breaks into a house like he did and acted as he did is to be feared. I don't let lady friends of mine be insulted by men. I never have and I never expect to at the age of seventy-nine. I am physically able to take care of a situation of that kind, and I don't think there should be a fistfight of that character in Miss Newberry's house." He sued them for $15,000 more and asked for a restraining order to keep them off her property, asserting she was afraid of them. Herwig pointed out to the court that "Cohen and Clark weigh a quarter of a ton and are over six feet."

In the beginning Monarch's lawyer-founder Paul J. McGarvey handled legal matters. But in June 1964 Cohen had hired as Monarch's attorney and resident agent one of Washington's prominent civic leaders, a black woman, Mrs. Margaret Haywood. Mrs. Haywood is now a member of the D. C. City Council, appointed by Lyndon B. Johnson in 1967 and reappointed by President Richard M. Nixon in 1971. Mrs. Haywood said that she met Cohen because one of her clients was having trouble over a Monarch contract. Subsequently she became Monarch's legal representative, taking depositions, handling court settlements, prosecuting cases to collect on contracts long after Monarch was out of business. Her appearance on behalf of Monarch was duly noted by the victims of her own race whom she pressed for payment; many make reference to "that colored lady lawyer." And it is said that her longtime association with Monarch diminished her reputation among those who were aware of the company's fraudulent activities.

Mrs. Haywood, when asked for an interview:

"I think it would be improper to discuss Monarch, but I will say that whatever the inner workings of Monarch were, I had nothing to do with. I represented them in litigation only."

As Monarch's corporation lawyer, Mrs. Haywood filed an answer to Herwig's charges against Monarch, denying them all and assuring the court Miss Newberry had nothing to fear from three respectable businessmen. It is said that Colonel Herwig's legal motions were sometimes out of order, and his facts seemed outrageous though they were correct; and his motions were often denied by the court. But he did not let up. He kept up a private investigation of Monarch, pursuing his case until ill health prevented him from doing so. He took complaints to the FHA, local and federal officials, civic organizations, and later even enlisted the help of one of the Monarch salesmen, Robert Freed, who had sold Bessie Newberry the unwanted towne house front. Freed later proved instrumental in the downfall of Monarch.

Remarkably, L. J. H. Herwig had figured out the thrust of

Monarch's operation months before anyone else, but very few persons took him seriously. As Maribeth Halloran, Neighborhood Legal Services lawyer with eighty Monarch clients, said recently: "Colonel Herwig is the only lawyer in town who saw fit to file. This feisty old guy went to the belly of the whale; he sued everybody. But in 1964 nobody had put the whole Monarch case together, nobody knew how much of a fraud it was, and other lawyers thought he was crazy."

On November 1, 1964, Monarch received its first bad publicity. A young reporter at the Washington *Post*, Rasa Gustatis, reported Bessie Newberry's suit against Monarch, interviewed Cohen, a number of his customers, and several of Washington's civic leaders. The article was the first to alert the community about Monarch's activities, but it went unheeded by many. It ran under a six-column headline in the paper's City Life section and took up the top half of a page. It bore down heavily on Cohen's urban renewal pretensions and carried vehement denials by black leaders the Reverend Edward A. Hailes and the Reverend Channing E. Phillips that they had ever endorsed Monarch's work or given permission for their photographs to be used in sales kits.

Cohen was to say later that the press "twisted everything I ever said." Stanley Silver recalled that the story "made Monarch look bad." Clark was especially disturbed by the repudiation from the Reverend Hailes and the Reverend Phillips and subsequently called in sales kits, containing their photos, for destruction. R. Ellwood Wilson said he did not remember whether he saw the article or not. The impact of its revelations are unknown. In any event, Citizens Building and Loan Association continued to shell out the weekly checks to Nathan Cohen. Jefferson Federal continued to do business with Monarch through broker Earl Lapin. Mrs. Margaret Haywood continued to defend Monarch in civil suits and was soon, in December, to institute suits against Monarch customers who refused to pay. The story, plus growing complaints against Monarch, however, ruffled Monarch principals enough to incite them to take a counteroffensive. Monarch hired a public relations firm, Lewis, Dobrow & Lamb, at a retainer of $2000 a month "to tell Monarch's side of the story." It was a move that was to hasten Monarch's downfall considerably.

The agency, under the guidance of Delmar Beman, public relations man, planned an advertising campaign for Monarch attacking government urban renewal and extolling itself.

On January 11, 1965, Monarch ran a full-page advertisement, costing some $5000, in the Washington *Post*:

Washington Has a Choice:
URBAN RENEWAL
OR URBAN REMOVAL?

Read the remarkable story of the American Towne House, a private urban renewal program not affiliated with the Federal or D. C. Governments.

At its present stage of development, the Federal Urban Renewal program stands condemned by most responsible authorities as an abysmal failure. Incredibly, more dwellings have been demolished than have been con-

structed, and each new undertaking is accompanied by the anguished cries of displaced persons, dislocated businesses, and destroyed communities.

To date there has been more urban removal than urban renewal. Is there any single answer to this complex and critical problem? Perhaps not. But right here in Washington, D. C., one private business organization, the Monarch Construction Corporation, has created an exciting, economical, and exceptionally effective program of urban renewal that accomplishes many of the government's objectives, while overcoming most of the usual objections.

After 18 months of successful operation and reconstruction we believe the facts about this little-known urban renewal effort should be made familiar to the Washington public:

Through private enterprise and ingenuity it [*Monarch*] *has at remarkably low cost to each participant restored and rejuvenated the appearance of nearly 400 family dwellings in Washington, without cruelly dislocating families from their familiar environment. In fact, current demand for the American Towne House is running far in excess of our ability to provide immediate services. In its 18 months of existence, the American Towne House Program has proved to be a most important force in reconstruction and renewal in our nation's capital. The American Towne House guarantees all materials, construction, and workmanship for one full year. Indeed we invite any of our participants with any problem, no matter how minor, to inform us at once.*

—*Excerpted from the ad.*

The ad also ran in the Washington *Daily News* and the Washington *Afro-American.* Monarch scheduled $15,000 more for advertising, and the following month, on February 20, ran a full-page ad, again in the *Afro-American,* purporting to explain "The Economics of Urban Renewal." The ad reported that during 1964 Monarch had created $2,149,500 in new first mortgages in the District and an additional $300,000 worth of FHA loans. This ad was followed up by one on March 23, 1965, in the Washington *Daily News.* Beman had clipped the January 11 ad and sent it to every Congressman. As expected, many replied. Beman then used their letters in another full-page ad:

> *WE WENT TO THE CONGRESS OF THE UNITED STATES WITH THE STORY OF THE AMERICAN TOWNE HOUSE PROGRAM. THE RESPONSE WAS GRATIFYING AND OVERWHELMING.*

Splayed around the page were reproductions of letters from Senators William Fulbright, Allen Ellender, Frank Lausche, Herman E. Talmadge, John G. Tower, William Proxmire, Joseph Tydings, Harrison A. Williams, Peter Dominick, and a number of members of the House of Representatives. Many of the letters were innocuous: "Thank you for calling this to my attention." Others went further:

> *I want to thank you for sending me a copy of your recent advertisement in the Washington* Post. *I had noticed the ad when it appeared and was impressed by the message it gives. I certainly feel that the renewal of such areas of Washington as Georgetown and Capitol Hill demonstrate*

there is an important role for private enterprise in the renewal of our cities. Indeed in my opinion private enterprise must play the major role with Federal Assistance supplementing this role.

Yours sincerely,
Senator Joseph Tydings,
Maryland

You certainly are to be congratulated on your program of sparking urban renewal through private enterprise. Our Nation's Capital will be the great beneficiary of this program, emphasizing once again that private enterprise can still do the job.

Clark McGregor,
Congressman from Ohio

I think you have done a marvelous job.

Senator Peter Dominick,
Colorado.

The program your advertisement describes seems like the kind of enlightened and eminently practical approach which private enterprise should be offering to deal with these immensely difficult problems. The more companies like yours, the lower our bills will be for federally aided urban renewal and public housing projects.

Senator Harrison Williams,
New Jersey

Monarch's ads, in Cohen's word, "backfired." Perhaps buoyed by an unprecedented sales record and new money, Cohen misjudged the amount of antagonism against Monarch. Instead of attracting supporters to the company, the ads tapped a reservoir of anger that had been steadily growing.

The brazenness of Monarch in advertising itself was too much for many of its enemies, especially its commercial exploitation of the United States Congress. Reaction was swift: D. C. Urban Renewal, a government agency, which had received numerous complaints against the company, now put one of its staff, Alma Scurlock, on special assignment to investigate Monarch. The Capitol Hill Restoration Society, a group of citizens which had been collecting information on Monarch, asked the Senate and House District Committees for a Congressional investigation of Mr. Cohen and associates. The peripatetic Colonel Herwig personally went knocking on Congressmen's doors to warn them about Monarch. Home-improvement contractor John H. Haas, that lone voice in previous years, was now joined by D. C. Urban Renewal and the Redevelopment Land Agency (another urban renewal arm of government) in urging Licenses and Inspection to refuse Monarch a license for 1965. Julian Green, once again, ignored the plea, and after perfunctory conferences with Cohen and Clark, renewed their licenses for the year. Several Congressmen were angered to see their letters used commercially, although Monarch's PR man, Del Beman, said he had cleared it with their staffs. Senator Frank Lausche inserted a statement of rebuttal in the *Congressional Record.* Senator Joseph Tydings was so chagrined that he later held hearings on home-improvement firms in the District, including Monarch.

*

One man saw the ads who was to cause Cohen the most immediate damage. He was Robert Freed, a former Monarch salesman, who had left the company after an argument with Cohen. Reportedly, Freed was angered over not receiving his proper commissions. Freed was the Mennonite salesman who had helped solicit a contract from Bessie Newberry and, since leaving Monarch, had helped Colonel Herwig with information about the company. Freed, upon seeing the first ad, called Colonel Herwig, and on that very day L. J. H. Herwig wrote a letter to the FHA which intrigued them considerably more than others he had been sending.

January 11, 1965

Honorable Philip N. Browstein
Commissioner, Federal Housing Administration

Request: A certain person who has worked in perpetration of this racket [Monarch] will reveal facts thereof if granted immunity.

I have promised not to disclose person's identity pending your action upon this request. He states he is "particeps criminis" and that he has been threatened with violence and other acts of reprisals and he is unable to furnish bail.

Please acknowledge receipt of this communication without delay.

L. J. H. Herwig

According to Herwig, Robert Freed felt he, like other salesmen, might be criminally liable for FHA violations, namely, "split financing"—taking proceeds from both a new first mortgage and a second FHA mortage-loan for the same job, which was clearly illegal, but which Monarch did consistently. Freed was not given formal immunity (although he was never prosecuted); nevertheless, on January 27, Freed met with two FHA officials in the office of Alfred Hantman, then an assistant U.S. attorney for the District of Columbia. Freed in the following weeks gave information about the inner workings of Monarch to both Hantman and the FHA and obtained corroboration of his charges from another former Monarch salesman, Kent Damkoehler, who also cooperated with the government. Damkoehler managed to salvage and turn over to Hantman one of Monarch's sales kits which Clark had scheduled for destruction. Clark had been exceedingly nervous when he learned Alfred Hantman was interested in Monarch, for Hantman was the prosecutor who had convicted Clark eight years earlier.

Cohen was to say later: "The investigations wouldn't have started had it not been for those damn ads." He was probably right. On February 9, 1965—three weeks after the appearance of the first ad—the FHA began an investigation of Monarch. And about the same time, Hantman set up a file: *US vs. Cohen, et al.*

THE FHA's INVESTIGATION of Monarch was conducted by John R. Sweeney, an experienced man, who, Monarch claimed, was trying to smear them. Cohen and Clark visited customers Sweeney had talked to and induced some to sign statements against him, saying that they were happy with the work and that Sweeney was a "troublemaker." The two also scrambled around to get endorsements of Monarch to thwart the investigation. The files of Monarch contained letters written in the recognizable hand of Myrvin C. Clark and signed by supposedly pleased owners of the towne house front.

Cohen, Clark, and Greenfield had known the FHA investigation was impending and had tried to stop it through their public relations counsel, Del Beman. Beman in early February tried but failed to get an appointment for Cohen with Robert C. Weaver, then administrator of the Housing and Home Finance Agency of which the FHA was a part. Beman wrote Weaver that "certain economic interests who don't want Monarch's program to succeed are attempting to use the power of one of the agencies under your office as a way to stop it." As the number of complaints against Monarch grew, Cohen tried to deflect them by picturing Monarch as a young, struggling company under persecution. He claimed that fake charges against Monarch were drummed up by real-estate speculators who had planned to buy and resell the houses Monarch was renovating and by jealous bureaucrats who wanted urban renewal to themselves. They are trying to "bury a little company" and using the FHA to do it, proclaimed Cohen.

Sweeney's investigation ended all speculation about the legitimacy of the complaints officials had been hearing for nearly two years. By interviewing former Monarch salesmen Robert M. Freed and Kent Damkoehler and ten Monarch customers with FHA-insured loans at Citizens, Sweeney documented a pattern of operation: Monarch had jacked up prices as high as possible without regard for the value of the work; had rewritten contracts; induced sales through false promises to consolidate debts; obtained signatures on documents through misrepresentations; falsified credit applications by failing to disclose all the borrower's debts; submitted completion certificates before work was finished; practiced "split financing"—taking funds for the same work from both a new first mortgage and a second-mortgage loan at Citizens—a violation of FHA regulations.

Investigators established that much of the work was left unfinished, or of poor quality, and, perhaps most significantly of all, documented for the first time the extent of the overcharge by Monarch and the staggering debts the company had placed on those who could least afford them.

*

Robert A. and Minerva Beasley	
1369 Spring Road, N. W.	
Original indebtedness	$11,945.72
Financing FHA Loan	837.45
Payments to Monarch	6,900.00

From FHA Loan $3500	
Note of Beasley to Monarch $3400	
Final indebtedness	$19,683.17

The work performed on the Beasleys' home was examined by William W. Prentice, Construction Examiner, FHA, Washington, D. C. Prentice made the following evaluation of Monarch Construction Corporation's work:

Demolition	$ 75
Towne House Front	
Alum siding w/furring & foil 20′ x 11′ = 220 s/ft @ 1.07	235
21′ W.I. Rail—7.00 per ft.	147
Shutters 8 pair @ 18.00 pair	144
Wood Window Sash 6/6 7 pr. @ 75.00	525
Concrete Cheek Walls—2′ x 21′ @ 2.00 sf	84
Front Door, Hdwre, One-Way Glass Frame, Fascia & Storm Dr.	246
Pair Coach Lights, Incl. Outlets & Switch	44
Painting Ext. Brick Wall on Alley & Front	250
Total cost	1750
Gen.O.H. [overhead] 15%	263
	2013
Profit 40%	805
Total Cost & Gen. OH & P	$2818

Note: Promise was made that kitchen and dining room ceilings would be repaired. This was not done. The front door was defective and was replaced but never painted. Paint was delivered for interior painting by owner.

From the above financial analysis and the construction examination, the following appears to have occurred:

Payments to Monarch	$6900.00	
FHA Evaluation of Work	2818.00	
Overcharge by Monarch		$4082.00

*

Robert Beasley was a laborer earning $95 a week, his wife a cleaning woman, bringing home $150 a month. They had five children. Their monthly house payments increased from $184.42 to $301.43, "an amount they cannot possibly continue to pay as is evident from their credit application," noted Sweeney. Cohen had also promised to pay off Beasley's car payments of $900, and cemetery lot, which he did not do; the finance company threatened to repossess the car.

The others in the investigation were overcharged, according to FHA appraisers:

Tommie and Annie M. Bacoti	$2343.09
William F. and Juanita Campbell	1405.00
Emerson and Roxie Davis	1273.00
Gentle Lee and Ella Mae Felder	596.59
William A. and Dorothy Mattingly	2202.15
Nathel J. and Maxine Tait	293.33
Marshall H. and Hazel Thomas	1446.63

In two instances FHA property appraisers decided Monarch did not charge unreasonably, but some authorities quarrel with the FHA cost assessment, believing a profit allowance of

40 per cent is excessive. Also, the actual cost of the towne house front in labor, materials, and overhead, as shown in the Towne House Construction Company records, was usually about $1250, whereas FHA allowed a cost of $2000. Thus, FHA's estimates of overcharges are low.

Even so, the overcharge figures are not an accurate measure of the harm. For homeowners not only paid for the overcharge, but also for interest to Citizens, usually $837.45, and the "closing costs" (the fees for insurance, title search, appraisal, Lapin's commission) of the new first mortgages, which they had been better off without and which served only to enrich Monarch, Lapin, the bank granting the loan and the title company. The "closing costs" on each loan were about $1000, lost to the homeowner, says Inspector Jason Souder, just as surely as if he "had dropped it down a sewer." It was a clear case of generating wasteful debt.

Thus, a truer indication of harm is a comparison of the customers' original indebtedness and final indebtedness, as taken from Sweeney's report: (These figures, however, do not include the 6½ per cent interest on the new first mortgage loans to be paid through the years.)

	Original Indebtedness	Final Indebtedness	Difference
Bacoti	$3,797.16	$11,236.75	$7,439.59
Beasley	11,945.72	19,683.17	7,737.45
(Beasley is the only one in the investigation who did not receive a new first mortgage).			
Campbell	7,791.04	14,739.95	6,948.91
Davis	6,431.08	11,756.18	5,325.10

Diggins	7,782.03	13,837.45	6,055.42
Felder	7,479.71	12,376.32	4,896.61
Mattingly	3,654.30	11,337.45	7,683.15
Riddick	4,920.04	9,503.53	4,583.49
Tait	9,365.38	14,337.45	4,972.07
Thomas	9,005.37	15,837.45	6,832.08

For these prices—ranging from $7683 to $4583—customers usually bought little more than a towne house front, sometimes completed, more often not. Only the Digginses seem to have been given substantial interior improvements, including a new vinyl floor and kitchen cabinets. The Bacotis got, according to FHA estimates, about $400 in wiring and painting and the Campbells got a new furnace valued by FHA at $375, as did the Mattinglys.

*

On April 15 John R. Sweeney completed his report on Monarch, and on May 11 the FHA put Monarch Construction Corporation and its president, former Baltimore businessman Nathan H. Cohen, on its precautionary measures list.

To: Qualified Title I Lending Institutions
Re: Monarch Construction Corporation
President, Nathan H. Cohen

This is notice to you that this Agency is in possession of certain information concerning the operations of the subject of this letter as they pertain to property improvements financed with loans subsequently reported for insurance under Title I of the National Housing Act, indicating that the subject has not conducted his opera-

tions in accordance with standards and practices consistent with the purposes and objectives of the FHA Property Improvement Program. . . .

C. E. Childs, Jr.
Director.

The directive virtually prohibited Citizens from doing any more business with Monarch. R. Ellwood Wilson later told investigators that Cohen and Greenfield urged Citizens to continue to buy contracts without FHA-guaranty, but "that was impossible." The noontime trips to Citizens, the lunches, the processing of the papers, the checks to Cohen, ended abruptly, a fact which C. Edwin Kline, president, seems to have regretted. On May 26, 1965—two weeks after the FHA's action—C. Edwin Kline wrote this letter to Marvin Greenfield:

Dear Marvin:

I haven't been able to get in touch with you recently, but I would still like for sometime in the future if you, Ellwood, Nathan, and I could sit down and talk a little bit only in the interest of being of help, even though we may not get any more business from you. I think a great deal of you guys and your ability, and I hesitate to be presumptuous in suggesting perhaps I could be of some assistance in making suggestions because I am not experienced in your line of business.

However, you have a gold mine at your doorstep and I would like to see you capitalize on it.

Cordially yours,
Ed

In July, R. Ellwood Wilson was fired, a fact which he said later did not embitter him. He said he "never got along with

Kline anyway," and that "because of my drinking problem I could understand their asking me to leave." Assistant FHA Commissioner Harry A. Finney was later to tell a Washington attorney that he was "certain Wilson was so under the influence of Cohen that he involved himself in a number of stupid transactions."

Although Monarch remained in business for a few more months, the FHA's action foreshadowed the end. The sales books following the FHA blacklisting show a decided decline. With FHA financing dried up, Cohen sold some notes to private investors and to Atlas Financial Corporation. Clark left his position as sales executive and went out on the street selling. Almost all of the last customers' names are followed by the notation, "MCC deal," for Myrvin Cochran Clark. Clark, however, still conducted a once-a-month sales meeting in the evening, and on June 1 a Congressman with an interest in urban renewal was asked to speak: the man from Texas, John P. Dowdy. Dowdy, a Democrat, who had served in Congress since 1952, was given a $500 honorarium for his speech. Subsequently Myrvin Clark began dropping by the Congressman's office for chats about his own problems and Dowdy's coming primary campaign in the spring of 1966, which promised to be a tough one and for which he needed money.

By July 1965 Cohen and Clark showed up less frequently at Monarch's offices.

The most tenacious was Greenfield, understandably, because of his large investment. He tried single-handedly to keep the office going. On August 12 Greenfield and his one-time friend Daniel Pope got in a fistfight in Cohen's office over the

Roseanne Realty commissions from the new first-mortgage settlements. Pope said Greenfield hit him first, and Greenfield said: "He hit me with his fists; my glasses went off and I hit him back." According to witnesses, the two wrestled about thirty seconds on the floor while Cohen looked on. Greenfield was later found guilty of assault and fined $100.

Soon afterward the names of customers disappear from the ledger sheets entirely. The offices were virtually deserted after the fight, according to Pope, and one of the last hangers-on was Mrs. Thelma Cohen. In late August Monarch was evicted from its offices at 10111 Colesville Road, and somewhat later Cohen, Greenfield, Stanley Silver, and Jack Gordon, to whom Monarch was heavily in debt, met to divide up what was left of the company. Greenfield took some of the customers' notes himself, but most of them, with Cohen's signed approval, were turned over to Jack A. Gordon for collection as absolution from the debt.

*

Around the same time—on September 22—Myrvin Clark made a trip to Atlanta, where he met Congressman John Dowdy and gave him a briefcase containing $25,000 in cash as a "campaign contribution." Cohen at the time was "absolutely terrified" by the investigation then being carried on by Assistant U.S. Attorney Alfred Hantman. "I was sure I was going to be indicted," he said later. Hoping that Congressman Dowdy could use his influence to forestall prosecution, Cohen borrowed $16,000 from his mother, Thelma, $4000 from a former Monarch salesmen, Julius "Jack" Levitt, and $5000 from his brother-in-law Stanley Silver, all of whom drew out the funds in $100, $50, and $20 bills. Cohen, his wife, Roseanne, his mother, Levitt, and former Monarch salesman Daniel Pope all recorded the serial numbers on the bills before they were packed in the attaché case. Clark and Levitt then in cloak-and-dagger fashion took separate planes to Atlanta where Dowdy on that day had a stopover during a flight from the District of Columbia to Shreveport, Louisiana, where he was giving a speech. (Cohen said he sent Levitt too because "I didn't really trust Clark with $25,000 of my money without anyone seeing it delivered!") Levitt, who says he was actually entrusted with carrying the money, then passed the attaché case to Clark in the airport who passed it on to Dowdy as he deplaned. Cohen says he preferred to have the money passed in Atlanta where there was less chance of someone's seeing and that Clark, who made the arrangements, said Dowdy had insisted on it. Dowdy later said, according to Cohen, that the rendezvous in Atlanta was just "Myrvin's theatrics."

At the time, Dowdy's subcommittee of the House District Committee was holding more hearings on urban renewal, and Cohen urged that he be allowed to testify before the committee about Monarch's activities in return for immunity from prosecution. Dowdy reportedly said that was not possible, but after September 22 he did take an active interest in Monarch. He met with FHA officials and prosecutors from the U. S. Attorney's office to discuss their investigation of Monarch. In October John Dowdy's subcommittee subpoenaed all "the files, records, memoranda, and complaints in the possession of the Department of Licenses and Inspections relating to Nathan

Cohen and the Monarch Construction Corporation." When the files were returned, according to director C. H. Nottingham, who had thought to make a list of them, about thirty of the documents were missing. Clark later said that Dowdy turned over to him copies of a number of government documents, including the FHA's report on Monarch.

On October 6, 1965, Nathan Cohen performed his last act as president of Monarch. He mailed the company's home-improvement contractors license number 288 to the Licenses Department with the note: "Monarch does not contemplate doing any more business in the District of Columbia." The company was officially defunct after a little more than two years of operation. And everyone was safe—for a while. Until someone in the Justice Department decided that the crime of bribing a Congressman was of more importance than robbing the poor of four and a half million dollars.

HUNDREDS OF Washington's poor were entrapped by Monarch; precisely how many is unknown. Clark states that at least 1000 towne house fronts were sold. Records in the U. S. Attorney's office show that between January and August 1965 alone, at the height of business, Monarch had about 750 customers. Earlier sales records are incomplete. And many of the families that dealt with Monarch can no longer be located. Some were forced out of their homes and the city and are now untraceable. In early 1971 Seymour Glanzer, Assistant U. S. Attorney, estimated that only 150 of the families victimized by Monarch had been found. Some victims to this day do not know they were cheated, and others, for whom the pain was too great, have chosen to try to forget. It is evident, however, from those still locatable that Monarch left in its wake a time of terror and personal destruction for many. Which persisted for years. For some up until the present.

Some who saw what was happening to them tried desperately to get help and often failed. Through the years some did manage to get lawyers and extricate themselves to an extent, but often only after they had paid thousands of dollars and were financially exhausted. Such is the nature of the crime that it did not end even when Monarch finally went out of business. The financial institutions that kept Cohen in business for so long by buying notes from him continued to press for collection, as the law allowed, long after Monarch's offices closed. It was a process of slow and painful extortion that ate away at people's futures and hopes.

Bankers and the lawyers who serve them are not commonly regarded by society as thugs. But their legal weapons of extortion are more formidable, more insidious, and more capable of producing violent results than those available to the common thief. They have at their disposal property confiscation—sometimes without court review—garnishment of wages, other court judgments, and as a concomitant, the unbridled use of *threats* of foreclosure and other legal actions which are often most persuasive of all.

Washington's poor paid and are still paying. They paid because they were forced to pay: a few under court order, others under duress, either actual or implied. They borrowed, sacrificed the needs of themselves and their children, depleted their savings if they had any, used retirement monies, took extra jobs, lived off the charity of friends and relatives. They paid: out of the pensions, Social Security, earnings from the menial jobs most of them held.

Alma Shepard, now dead, her two adult daughters, Jimmie Brewster and Lillie Jackson, Second Street, S.E. The quotations, unless otherwise noted, are from Lillie Jackson.

> "So they came around and they showed us some pictures of the house, some beautiful pictures naturally. My mother was old; she was eighty-two at the time. She was the sole owner of the house. So he told us, 'Well, it's not a contract, we jus getting up some names in the neighbor-

hood. So I said, 'How much are you gonna charge?' So he said, 'We aren't putting no prices right now. We just want to get some names together. So to see how much a workman can get done, you know, and then if it's worth our time we'll be back.' He was *so* smart. He was a medium-height man, nice-looking young fellow, but I forget his name. I guess he signed his name on the contract, but I don't know whether we did or not. We was dumb at the time.

"So he got to talkin. My mother saw the pictures, you know, she flipped. Because she wanted to get the pretty house for us because I think she realized she was getting older and she jus wanted us to have a pretty house. She wanted it remodeled for us, you know, wanted the towne house. Before, it was gray brick, beautiful paint, hadn't been long painted, either. But she got excited over this kind of—what did they call it?—she wanted it fixed in a towne house. She liked that picture. I said, 'Mama, you better think about it.' She said, 'I jus want it fixed like this. I jus want it to look like this.' She got excited over the little black shutters, and you know, we just wanted to please her. So she wanted it. But he said, 'It's not a contract, not a contract, Mrs. Shepard.' So Mama signed. So I said, 'I don't know whether we should sign or not.' So he said, 'The signature don't mean anything.' And I'm dumb. I didn't think my signature meant anything, either. So we signed it—like idiots. Because Mama had already signed it, so he say, 'It don't make any different whether you sign or not. We've got the main name, your mother's name.'

"So we signed it. So we went off to work the next day. We come home from work and my mother said some man had came here and asked her for the contract. And when I looked at the contract, I said, 'What's this $3800 doin here!' Mama was old, was feeble-minded, I guess—you know how old people get. So I said, 'What's this for, what'd they put this here for?' They got us hooked. I didn't have no idea what it would cost. I was just completely in the dark. I thought maybe it might be about $1500, which I was willing to pay that much. We knew we had to pay something; we knew they wouldn't do it for nothing. So when I saw that, I said, 'For Chrissake, that's $4000 almost!' You know, $3900 is three thousand nine hundred dollars.

"So they came and they get to work, and then come talk to us, and the next day they had a board across the front. They just put it up there, I don't know why, but I guess there was some technical reason they put it there—they had a reason—so I said, 'Well, Mama, the man said it wasn't a contract, why they have this thing up on the top here?' So she says, 'I don't know. I don't know it was out there. Just stuck off to the top out there.' But they had us hooked already cause they had our names.

"So anyway, they came and did the work, and they jus messed it up, jus slopped it up; they didn't care how they did it. They was gonna give us the red Chinese door. He said you can see out but they can't see in, and blah, blah, blah, blah. So he was not even going to give us the red door. I say, 'You know you promised in the contract that you was going to give us the red Chinese door, where is it?' So they had to send a man back to put the Chinese door. We had to *make* them do everything.

"Then these people come at night and had us sign these papers. A whole lot of papers. Mr. Cohen, Mr. Anderson, they was the two that night. The reason I knew this man was Cohens, he said he was president of this thing. He set right here; he had the whole couch down he was so fat. And I didn't believe it. I said how can this man be president of Monarch Company, because his pants was torn in the back, but absolutely he was the Pres-i-dent, because I saw it.

"And they set up there and they look me square in the eye, you know, when they say people is crooked they can't look you in the eye, don't tell that. He looked me dead in the eye, hypnotized me, ya know. He looked just like you see on movies, these big gangsters, jus what he looked like; for a moment there I was a little scared. They put the X where we all supposed to sign our name. And we kept a-signing, and then my mother said—I don't know, something must of hit her. Mama said, 'I'm not signing another paper, I have a feeling I've already signed enough papers.' But wouldn't you know it, come to me after all this, we signed the wrong papers. We were signing the contracts, supposed to be signing the contracts. They asked for the first contract back, so we gave it to them like nuts. Then first thing we know, they sent us a bill out here. The Citizens bank had sent us a book—some books for $4000 something. So I said, 'Well, that's the first time I ever heard of Citizens bank in my life. When I got this book.'

"I tell you how we got this house. World War II was over, we all chipped in and bought the house. We come up here in '39. Before that we were sharecroppers in South Carolina. Didn't own nothing, my poor papa didn't own nothing, with five little hungry children. That's all my poor papa ever owned, and a whole lot of hard work—blood, sweat, and tears. Mother worked up until she just couldn't work no longer, bless her heart, she worked *so* hard, my father too. And I haven't been playing my lifetime neither. I started to work at nine years old and I been getting up ever since.

"So we all chipped in together, our little wartime money, ya know. I worked at the NLRB and Jimmie at the Pentagon. And we worked like slaves to get the little money for the down payment; it was $800. The whole family, me and my mother and our three sisters, all of us. We all signed the house over to my father. Long as my father lived, the house was his, so after my father died, we signed it all over to my mother. They never owned a home before this. First one, so that's why they was so shook up over it, ya know. They'd worked so hard and now they figure they had em a little home, they had reached the Holy City. So naturally they was glad, cause they had worked so hard all their life and they had bought the home and they was kinda happy over it. So after Mama died, the house come to us and our sisters, but just us two live here now.

"My mother had a sick spell in '64. I think the same year that they come here—but she kind of got better and got around a little bit, and then she got sick again in '66. Must have been around the spring of the year, about April, and she jus kept gettin worse and worse, and she died in July. And I think worrying about this house problem, that's what shortened her life. She worried, yes, indeed. Because she loved this old barn, she loved this house. And I say that had to kind of shorten her life span because she worried more than she wanted us to know. . ."

It was December 1964, just before Christmas, when Alma Shepard put her feeble hand to a contract with Monarch. Later she refused to sign, although as it turned out she and her two daughters had already signed a promissory note payable to Monarch which was sold to Citizens and now bears an amount due of $4337.42. Earl Lapin attempted to pressure Alma Shepard and her daughters into negotiating a new first mortgage so more money without their knowledge could be extracted. But by that time Lillie Jackson realized the deceit. She had asked the Perpetual Building Association, where they had their first mortgage, to raise it. And when Perpetual's appraiser saw the work on the house he told her they had been soundly cheated. "He said, 'You all been taken by a bunch of crooks,' and I'll tell you I got sick. Cause they haven't done anything for all that money. He said, 'Those shutters out there, those people get them a dollar a hundred, they're so cheap.' So by the time Mr. Earl came over here, we had already discovered they was selling us down the river, so I didn't even talk to him. By then I was so mad, I say, 'I don't want to talk to you no more. I'm not going to talk to anybody about that Monarch Company; just get out of here.'" There was an angry scene, and Lapin told them he would get his money if he had to sell their house, because, he said, they had already signed a second mortgage. Which they hadn't. They had stopped short.

In February the payment book with the detachable coupons for $72 a month for five years arrived from Citizens Building and Loan Association. Never having heard of Citizens before and believing they had signed no promissory note for $4337.42 for an FHA-insured loan, Lillie Jackson had the good sense to take the matter immediately to a lawyer. Flatly, he told her not to pay it and she didn't. She made one complaint to Citizens, claiming she had not signed a promissory note, and she heard nothing more. Until September 10, 1965. On that fall day at precisely 3:48 in the afternoon a United States marshal knocked at the door and handed the following paper to the old woman who was Alma Shepard:

SUMMONS

Alma Shepard
a/k/a Mrs. Jimmie Brewster
a/k/a Lillie Jackson

You are hereby summoned and required to appear personally or through an attorney at the office of the Clerk of this Court in Room 102 within twenty (20) days after service of this summons upon you . . . and to file an answer to the complaint which is herewith served upon you.

You are required to send a copy of your answer to the attorney for the plaintiff whose name and address are at the bottom hereof:

IMPORTANT: If you fail to appear and answer within the required time, judgment by default will be taken against you for the relief demanded in the complaint.

Citizens was suing them for $4337.45 plus $650.51 in attorney's fees and late charges of $14.40 together with costs of the suit.

"When we come home that day—I remember it was a gloomy fall day—Mama said, 'Well, we been summoned to court,' cause Mama was old, ya know, and she thought it was a big joke, but I knew then it was serious. She was just old and feeble like, she didn't really understand. So I

> looked at the summons and I said, 'We got to get a lawyer.' I said, 'Because, Mama, this summons is serious now, because they gonna make us pay. We got to answer the summons.' "

There were twenty days in which to answer the summons, and Lillie Jackson recalls that she took the summons in the next day or two to an attorney, John J. Spriggs. He didn't answer it. On October 5, 1965, a judgment by default was entered in the docket of the General Sessions Court (now Superior Court) for $5014.46—against Alma Shepard, Jimmie Brewster, and Lillie Jackson. They knew nothing about it. In the couple of times they asked their attorney, Spriggs, what was happening, they say, he assured them their case was "progressing."

In August of the following year another summons was sent to Mrs. Shepard—this time on a suit to foreclose on the house—but it went undelivered. For by this time Alma Shepard, as the U.S. marshal noted, was "deceased." With this information, Citizens' attorney Irving Turner, a small man with a shock of gray hair, known as a collection lawyer, decided on another course of action. It had been a year and four months of silence since Jimmie Brewster and Lillie Jackson had received the summons, and though they were uneasy at times about it, they assumed their lawyer must have disposed of it.

Then on February 23, 1967, Lillie Jackson, as usual, went to the linen room at the Harrison Hotel, where she worked as a maid, to pick up her two weeks' paycheck. The auditor handed her a "big white piece of paper." She asked what it was, and he told her it was a garnishment, an attachment of her wages from Citizens. At first she thought he was kidding, then she read it. "And I really, I'm telling you, I cried a river. Oh, Lord, I thought I could never stop crying. I made myself sick. Cause I just didn't think they could do that. All the time I thought I had a lawyer workin for me, and he wasn't doin a thing. And when I saw it was *real*, I said, 'Lord have mercy, here we are.' I said, 'These people *got* us, and it's too late to do anything about it. They got the garnishee on us.' "

Two weeks later her sister, Jimmie Brewster, who is a maid at the Ambassador Hotel, received notice that her wages too would be garnisheed, part of them sent every two weeks to Irving Turner at 608 Washington Building, until the debt of $5014.46 was paid off to Citizens Building and Loan for the towne house front, a dream now dead with their mother.

Lillie Jackson, a woman of great vitality and intelligence, was stunned, but she gathered up her papers again, with her courage, and took them to another lawyer. It was then for the first time that she learned her former attorney, John J. Spriggs, had not answered the summons she had put in his hands, that there was a court judgment against her and her sister for which the garnishments had been issued.

> "I think all of it is his fault, the whole thing. But some of it is my fault for signing the papers. Now I'm not blaming him for that. But for letting this judgment get on me, it's Mr. Spriggs's fault. They don't think about no poor folks. When you poor you jus out in the cold. I found out when you don't have any money, you can't even get a lawyer. You really left out. People say, 'Well, you should have took the summons to court yourself.' Well, I didn't know. That's why I got a lawyer."

John Spriggs was to say later that he thought he had answered the summons (which he clearly had not, according to the court records), but that also he considered it hopeless to fight the matter because Citizens was a "holder in due course."

> "We never seen a day in court. Never spent the first minute in court. Never had a chance to defend ourselves."

Lillie Jackson and Jimmie Brewster were at that time each taking home $54.90 a week from their jobs as hotel maids. Every payday a portion was withheld and credited by Irving Turner, Citizens' attorney, to their account. And the debt went slowly down:

Date	Payment	Balance
3/9/67	23.86	$4979.62
3/21/67	33.47	4946.15
4/7/67	26.47	4919.68
4/20/67	27.92	4891.76
5/8/67	36.24	4855.52
5/11/67	34.01	4821.51
6/8/67	21.96	4799.55
6/14/67	25.60	4773.95

As Lillie Jackson realized, they were now worse off than if they had paid in the beginning, for they now had even to pay $650 in attorney's fees for Mr. Turner. Her new attorney told her now that the judgment was recorded and the garnishment in effect; there was nothing to be done about it. Lillie Jackson was in despair and even decided to sell the house until she realized that after $5000 went to Citizens they would have little money left and no place to live. She chaffed under the injustice, watching hours of her hard work go to Citizens through peonage.

"Sometimes they was taking $16 from me, for just about three weeks, and I said, 'Well, I might jus as well go on welfare because I won't be able to live if you're going to take $16 for my garnishee and $12 and 90 some cents for the FICA.' I wasn't bringing home anything. So naturally I kind of felt like committing suicide, but I thought I can't do that. I couldn't do that, but I had to do a whole lot of praying to keep from crackin up.

"If I didn't believe in *something*, I think I'd a went up to the Calvert Street bridge and jumped *down*. Because I had to join this life study fellowship after they got this garnishee. Had to have somebody help pray for me, because my mind was getting messed up—unhuh—cause I couldn't sleep or eat. It seems just like a *burden* was on me. An I said, 'Oh, God, how long will it take us to pay $5000?' and when I'd think about it—if my heart is bad it came from that, maybe it's jus nerves. But I'll tell you it kinda got to me, you know. They sent me some prayers, and I would pray these prayers three times a day. And honest to God, it really did make me feel better. And I been feeling better ever since, try not even to think about it. I say, 'Well, who steals my money takes trash,' and all that, ya know, but then sometimes I go back in the woods and worry more. If they would take it off me, I know I would live twenty years longer.

June 27, 1971 "Every time I get my check I think about it. Today they took union dues out, $54.23 left. Fifty-four dollars, that's a heartbreaking thing, cause I tell ya, it's hard work, cleaning. And there are the other girls bringing home $60 some odd or $70, and oh, boy, I got to pay the same thing for food that they pay, plus I can't get no credit, know what I mean? No, no, I can't because of the garnishment. I can't buy anything; I have to pay cash for everything. And I'm not bringing home any cash. Can't get no credit unless I have somebody to co-sign. I don't even know whether I can get a co-signer. My stepson co-signed with me for food once, but I hate to keep bugging him every time I buy, it's kind of embarrassing, really. So I just wouldn't try to borrow the money cause I hate to be a nuisance bothering him to co-sign every time I buy something. So there are so many things I need that I can't buy, because I don't have no cash money to pay for it, so I have to do without.

"Then you get a little overtime and they come and get that too. Yes, they garnishee that too."

Mrs. Jimmie Brewster for a while had a job at night cleaning offices so she could have a little money for herself.

"They was takin so much of my money, because every time I make overtime on my day job they take that, but I figured by making a little bit extra money from my other job, maybe I could have that for myself. But it was around six hours at night, and after my day job it was too hard. I had to give it up.

"We can't get no other jobs, even if we wanted to. You know a lot of jobs don't allow no garnishee. That's why I'm staying where I'm at. And supposing they tear the building down, I'm out of a job, because a lot of jobs do not accept garnishees. So this is one of the things that's causing me a whole lot of problems. Cause I don't know how long they going have that hotel standing there.

> What's going to happen to me without a job? And I'm a little bit too old to be running from job to job."

For five years: 1967, 1968, 1969, 1970, 1971, scrubbing floors, sweeping, cleaning toilets, washing windows, making beds, emptying trash, wiping up after white-folks conventioneers, so the money could go to Irving Turner, attorney, hence to Citizens Building and Loan Association in Silver Spring, where R. Ellwood Wilson and Nathan Cohen used to have lunch those years ago while the papers that bound Lillie Jackson and Jimmie Brewster were being filled in. Where C. Edwin Kline, president, sat in his swivel chair and waved to Nathan and Marvin as they passed by.

*

The two women, now in their fifties, despair of ever being rid of the debt.

> "We've had three lawyers, but it seem none of them can help us. I asked the lawyer, "If it's money, talk to us,' because what little bit I've got I'm willing to spend, some of it anyway, to git rid of that garnishee. It's like a noose around my neck. Jus like I say, we had some work down on the house, and I know we owed those people some money, but we did *not* owe those people $5000, because they didn't do $5000 worth of work. Anybody come here and look at the work they know they didn't do $5000 worth of work.
>
> "I don't care whether we get any money back that we paid, maybe we overpaid, I don't care, jus as long as they *lift* that garnishee. I don't care if they don't give us a cent

back. They don't have to give me a dime, even if they overcharge me. Don't give it to me, jus' take the garnishee off and I feel some kind of happy. Oh, Lord, I think I'd go back to *church* and *join* again. Get up there and shout in the Aaaaa-men corner.

"I have always tried to be a honest person, ya know, work hard for my living and try to pay my bills, and I just don't think I *deserve* it. And I just wonder why *me*, of all people, why me. And look at the people who cheat and steal and do anything. Well, I guess it jus happen because I signed the wrong papers or something.

"Ya work *so* hard, and then they say they don't wanna see anybody on the welfare, ya work hard, and then look what they let people do to you. Jus seem like you work hard and somebody jus waiting to say, 'Hand it over,' in a different way, not with the gun in your side, but they got a pencil and paper, 'Sign your money away.' Enough to drive ya nuts if you let it. But I can't afford to let it. I can't give up [softly], got to go on living, just be careful next time, but I don't guess I have anything else to sign away. This is my last chance, because I'm not getting any younger, and you never know what's going to happen to you before you're through with this life, but this I'll never forget. I guess they will garnish my old-age pension."

"Just call it a lifetime garnishee. I guess it'll be all my life": Jimmie Brewster.

If you work for a man, in Heaven's name work *for him.*

If he pays you wages which supply you bread and butter, work for him; speak well of him; stand by him and stand by the institution he represents.

If put to a pinch, an ounce of loyalty is worth a pound of cleverness.

If you just villify, condemn, and eternally disparage —resign your position.

And when you are outside, damn to your heart's content, but as long as you are part of the institution do not condemn it.

If you do that you are loosening the tendrils that are holding you to the institution.

And at the first high wind that comes along, you will be uprooted and blown away and probably will never know the reason why.

—*The Restaurateur.*
—a sign in the linen room
where Jimmie Brewster works.

JAMES W. AND ELLEN THOMPSON, 11th Street, N.E., an elderly couple who were among the most vulnerable to Monarch: He was a veteran of World War I, drawing a pension of $78.75 monthly and Social Security of $103. She tried to run a small day-care home to supplement their income. In late 1964 they were told by a city housing inspector that they had code violations. There was no bathroom upstairs, the one downstairs was inadequate, walls needed painting, and the garage would have to be repaired or torn down. The next day a Monarch salesman was at the door (probably tipped off by an informant in the inspections department), offering to correct the code violations.

"And then in the meantime, while he was talking, he was talking about this Monarch front," recalls Thompson. And somehow James and Ellen Thompson understood that a towne house front was necessary to get their notes consolidated so they could afford the city-required repairs and the new front. At the time they were paying $117 out of their monthly checks of $181.75 for three mortgages on their house which they had owned since 1953.

*

"That old president, all of them Cohens came in," recalls Mr. Thompson. "There were about four or five of them came in, in the kitchen here, and they had a conference in there, and they was gonna do this and they was gonna do the other. Something to rectify these defects. That was the *main* thing. Other than that I wouldn't a talked to them." Mr. and Mrs. Thompson signed some papers, although they noticed they were blank. "But we didn't say nothing noway. We was so anxious to get something done. We was afraid they gonna condemn the house and make us move out. But after they left here they took them papers and filled them out like they wanted."

> "The madam—she wasn't much of a businesswoman, and you see, back when I went to school in the country in South Carolina they did more spellin than anything else, didn't do much readin. Tell you the truth, I went just about second grade, but from time to time I never stopped studying. I used to set down and listen to other people read and watch them close behind, and when they read that paper—I wouldn't know the words, but I could go pick up that paper and read it just like they did, and remember those words. That's how much remembrance I had. I used to fool a lot of people that way."

Sometime in the early spring of 1965 a couple of workmen came and put up about a five-foot-wide strip of white aluminum siding across the top half of the Thompsons' house, painted the brick a dark green which is now peeling, put up a small carriage lamp. No railing, no completion of the siding, no interior painting, no baths, no repairs to the garage. The house half covered by siding stands today as it did then when the workmen left. In March the Thompsons received a payment book from Citizens Building and Loan for an FHA loan of $4100 payable monthly at $68.29.

The Thompsons, elderly, retired, on a fixed income, were panicked. They realized that their debts had not been consolidated but increased. They now owed $185.54 a month—more than their income of $181.75 from the government checks. And their housing violations still existed. Mr. Thompson called Citizens and told them he couldn't possibly pay.

Citizens' response is shown by a memo to the file, dated March 25, 1965, from R. Ellwood Wilson:

Mr. Thompson called Mrs. Gaisband on the phone and stated that he realized he had a loan with this Association but would not be able to make his first payment which was due in May. Mrs. Gaisband called Mr. Small to listen in on this conversation from the extension. Mr. Thompson stated that his age is seventy-seven and his wife is about sixty.

He had been notified by the District of Columbia that his property would have to be improved because of code violations. The very next night a representative of Monarch Construction Corporation came out to see him. How Monarch found out about his code violations Mr. Thompson has no idea. The representative brought with him pictures of Roy Wilkins and Dr. Martin Luther King, and stated that the Thompsons were entitled to equal rights and they would have to fix up their property accordingly—comparable to white people. Mr. Thompson told Monarch that if it had to be done, to go ahead and do the work. He was told that his payments would be less with a new first trust [mortage] than they were before he had the work done. He owes on the following trusts:

$4000	1st trust
98	2nd trust
2800	3rd trust
$6898	Total

Mr. Thompson stated that he had very little education and felt he had been "tricked" by Monarch into signing those papers, and at this point we will have to foreclose because of his inability to make payments. . . . He has an income of a pension from the Army, Social Security, and his wife baby-sits occasionally.

Mr. Thompson is awaiting our decision.

The Thompsons lived in fear that Citizens would take their house. "Me and the madam went up there to Citizens. She did everything she thought would help us, cause I was old and she was old. Well, she died right after that, worried herself to death. She never got over it. And I lost my health. The Monarchs, you know, knocked me out. Cause after the payments was due, I missed about three or four, I got dizzy trying to get everything straightened out."

Thompson tried to borrow $800 from another bank to remedy the housing violations, but when the bank saw his indebtedness, they refused. With the building inspectors pressing, he borrowed about $300 from his son and his cousin, and with what little else he could scrape up "got a used basin and some other things at a wrecking place over at East Capitol," and installed the baths himself. It was not a professional job, but Thompson had worked thirty years in construction and knew a little about plumbing and electricity. He pleaded with the inspector to pass the work: "I said, 'I've already done the best I can,' and he gave me an okay."

Ellen Thompson wrote letters to everyone she could think of asking for help: local ministers, Senators, Dr. Martin Luther King, the President of the United States, the D. C. Licenses and Inspections Department, the FHA.

Dear Sir:

I am a citizen of the U.S. and so's my family. My husband and I are old people has payed off one trust on our house and we have been trying to buy for 12 years and with the inspector violations we could not get a loan, so the Monarch contractors came by and promise to get the loan through and put my notes higher than my retirement checks and charge me, and I have been fooled on what work they were going to do on the house they did not even finish the house and they got the money. Can you help me please.

Yours truly,
James and Ellen Thompson

Dear Mr. Thompson:

I am sorry to learn of the difficulty you are experiencing in refinancing your home. A local bank or Savings and Loan Company could offer useful guidance on meeting your problem. Fedrral agencies can only assist through accredited lending institutions.

Good luck!
Hubert H. Humphrey

Not everyone was insensitive to the Thompsons' pleas, however. Mr. Thompson recalls that the Reverend Walter E.

Fauntroy and the Reverend Edward A. Hailes of the NAACP and someone from Senator Edward Kennedy's staff came to the house and tried to help them. "All of them said it wasn't their line of work, but they would try to find somebody to help us." The Thompson's were directed to a private attorney who made a settlement with Citizens: they agreed not to foreclose if the Thompsons would pay off the debt at $25 a month instead of $68. After two years the sum was raised to $30.

Every month—as he has done for the past six years—Mr. Thompson, as he parcels out his small monthly income, makes out an envelope to Irving Turner, Citizens' attorney, in which he includes a check for a towne house front. Thompson says he has never missed a payment; so far he has paid about $2000. He is grateful to the lawyer who got him "straightened out" and to the people at Citizens who let him keep his house, even though he knows he was "fooled."

Thompson, his wife gone, now an old man in ill health, with a patch over one eye, slumped in a chair.

"I could have lost my house, but I tried to cooperate with them on everything. You know I'm an old man, I'm eighty-three years old, and I was scared to be messin around because I didn't want to be goin on the welfare and all that. I was afraid, yes, I was afraid they'd take my home, and I did the best I could. I don't want to be beggin. Time I've got to live here I want to live in peace. I know I've paid enough, and if I could get it stopped maybe I could live a little easier. Maybe get myself an extra drink of sody pop, maybe an extra pork chop."

*

If the money could not be extracted by threats, Citizens foreclosed, as Woodrow Campbell (an entirely different sort of man from the elderly James Thompson) discovered. Once a farmer in Carolina, he is a small muscular man in his forties with large hands, difficult to push around. He is the one who swore that if he ever met Cohen or Clark, he would beat them up.

In November 1964 he signed a contract for $3500 which Myrvin Clark assured him would not be binding until the work was finished; Clark promised by Christmas.

> "Cee-gar Clark, that's what he told me to call him, Cee-gar Clark, and that's what I always called him. He seemed like such a nice guy, he really did. I never thought the man would pull a stunt like that. A great big guy, coal-black hair, a nice-looking guy, talks nice. I had confidence in them, and I thought they was gonna do what they said. Just the way they talked, I *believed* them. You see, Clark told us he was from Georgia—he seemed like a Southern fella—and we was from the South too, and he just talked so confident we trusted him."

Some workmen came occasionally in late afternoon and stayed for a couple of hours. "They put in about six windows in six weeks." Eventually they put some pink siding on the front, painted a little of the side, erected a back porch that has crumbled beyond use, put up a back door that has fallen off, and tore down a drain spout which they never replaced. Half a dozen windows which they never installed are still in Campbell's basement. The house, like that of James Thompson, is a rather grotesque monument to the failure of Nathan Cohen's urban renewal program.

Campbell complained to Clark several times, and one evening Clark and Cohen came and urged Campbell to sign a completion certificate so they could get an "advance" from the bank to finish the work. Clark gave his word as a churchgoing Baptist that if Campbell signed there would be no more delays. Frustrated over months of construction and seeing no other way out, he did. Of course, he never saw the workmen again, nor Cee-gar Clark, nor Cohen. When Campbell called Monarch now, he got no response from Clark and was kept waiting on "hold" sometimes for half an hour until he hung up. So he quit calling. Then R. Ellwood Wilson at Citizens started calling Woodrow Campbell.

Campbell couldn't comprehend why he owed Citizens, who now held his note, when the work was not completed. He contended the bank should have checked the work before giving Monarch the money, and if they hadn't, it was their tough luck. Wilson retorted it was not Citizens' responsibility, and Campbell would pay or they would foreclose. Campbell thought it an idle threat and so unjust as to be unenforceable.

March 25, 1965

Memo to the file: Ellwood Wilson
Re: Woodrow Campbell

Mr. Campbell absolutely refuses to pay his bill until the job is completed and we can do whatever we wish. His employer speaks very highly of him. At this point, the account is uncollectible. Mr. Campbell said, "Monarch is the biggest crook in the city. . . ."

3/25. *Mr. Greenfield says Campbell will not let Monarch finish the work. We will have to foreclose on property.*

4/7/65. *Talked to Mr. Cohen and Greenfield about foreclosure. Will have to talk to Mr. Kline.*

Campbell heard no more, and then one evening in July a man rushed into his house with a newspaper clipping of the auction columns. Listed for sale, advertised by Thomas J. Owen and Sons, was Campbell's house. He was shaken and disbelieving. The next day he and his wife, Sarah, went to Silver Spring to see Wilson. Campbell knew then he would have to pay "for half a job" to save his house. At the time he had five children at home. Wilson agreed that if he promised to pay and brought his payments up to date, the auction would be halted. Sarah Campbell wrote a check for $216 for three back payments, and when it cleared the bank, Campbell recalls, "It was the best receipt we ever had."

On July 28 he was on call as an air-conditioner mechanic when a message came over his two-way communication radio in his truck that his house had been auctioned off. He was furious at the double cross as well as dazed. "Naturally, with five kids and no place to take them, I was worried to death. I had plenty of sleepless nights."

Furious, Campbell called Ellwood Wilson and "probably said some things I shouldn't of." Wilson informed Campbell that even though he had accepted the $216, the sale was out of his hands. Eventually Campbell through some strange circumstances managed to save his house. He got a lawyer who filed suit to prevent settlement of the sale: there is a thirty-day period after the sale before the deed is transferred. In this case, the deed was never given to the new owner. The high bidder for Campbell's property was Gerald Lillienfield, a speculator who buys second mortgages and numerous properties at foreclosure, then resells. He bid $5000 and gave a $500 deposit. However, as it turned out, Lillienfield was only a "straw buyer" for a close friend of his, one Marvin Greenfield, the very silent partner in Monarch who passed as "Mr. Stevens" and "Mr. Anderson." It is probable that Greenfield did not want to get involved in litigation that would expose his involvement with Monarch, so Lillienfield gave the property back. In a court settlement two years later, however, it was decreed that Campbell should pay Citizens $2000 for work he feels was worth $500 at most.

*

Despite reports from Monarch customers of uncompleted work, fraud, overpricing, irregularities in financing (Citizens' own records show complaints as early as January 1965, and some persons claim to have notified the bank prior to that), R. Ellwood Wilson and C. Edwin Kline continued to approve FHA loans through Monarch. It appears that Monarch's principals had almost dictatorial power at Citizens. When Wilson turned down a loan—perhaps because of a poor credit report—Marvin Greenfield would repeatedly call to protest. After refusing a loan for a couple named Gillson, Wilson sent a handwritten note: "Mr. Kline, I turned this down because of the man's age and income. Mr. Cohen and Greenfield felt it should be approved. What do you think?" It was initialed "OK" by Kline, and the loan was granted.

Many of the documents Cohen delivered to Citizens during his weekly visits were incomplete or in otherwise suspicious form. It is obvious from an inspection of the second mortages (deeds of trust) on record that many had dates crossed out and new ones written in, presumably in attempts to make them conform in time with other papers. Some of the completion certificates were undated, which Wilson later admitted was "irregular" and a violation of FHA requirements. Citizens also discovered that although they had paid Cohen for a certain job and possessed a signed completion certificate, the work had in fact not been finished. A handwritten memo by Wilson dated 4/14/65: "Wes [Small, an employee of Citizens] inspected the work again. Work is still not complete." Kline said later that about one out of five properties was inspected, although apparently most of these inspections did not take place until the spring of 1965 when complaints were too numerous to ignore.

Wilson also admitted in a letter to an attorney dated May 5, 1965, that: "We here at Citizens do feel that Monarch has overcharged in numerous instances; however, I don't know of any reason why that would prevent us from being a holder in due course on this note."

Most irregular of all, however, were the promissory notes which Cohen brought in; he says they were blank.

In startling testimony in June 1971, Cohen, testifying

under subpoena in the trial of Citizens vs. Clarence and Georgia Winters, asserted that Citizens demanded the promissory notes in blank, so they could be filled in later for the precise amount by Citizens. Cohen also stated to Winters' attorneys that Citizens backdated documents, notably letters for loan applications, in pretense of complying with FHA regulations.

Even Citizens' attorney Irving Turner was slightly taken aback by Cohen's disclosure. Turner has argued for years that Monarch customers were fully aware of the amounts they committed themselves to on the notes. Such a practice by Citizens does not automatically make the notes invalid, but raises additional questions about Citizens' knowledge of and complicity in the fraud. In any event, say attorneys representing Monarch victims, accepting blank notes, especially from unsophisticated persons, is an invitation to fraud and an irresponsible practice: to fill in what Citizens acknowledged to be inflated prices and then to rely on the legality of "holder in due course" for five years of extortion (the duration of the notes) against Washington's poor.

> *Sophisticated banking and finance organizations should have known what was taking place and should have discharged a duty to the public to offer them some kind of protection by not making it easy for fraudulent business activities such as Monarch to sell rotten instruments, become insolvent, and leave the poor homeowner to pay and suffer while the banking institutions feign innocence.*
>
> *—Paul Pascal and Noel Thompson, attorneys.*

After his testimony, Cohen, then with a beard, looking much like a young Walter Slezak, in a knitted shirt and belted suit, met Ellwood Wilson in the hallway. Wilson had also been subpoenaed to testify. "Sorry, guess I messed you up in there," said Cohen. Wilson, now in the leasing business, shrugged.

WHEN THOSE WHO had received FHA-insured loans through Monarch balked at paying the fraudulent debts, the FHA itself stepped in as a powerful collection agent against those it purported to protect. On behalf of lenders, the FHA sometimes sent what is known as its "preclaim" letter to those who were unable or unwilling to pay the FHA-insured debt Nathan Cohen had put upon them. The letter bore the seal of the United States and was strongly worded. Quite understandably, a person who received such a letter from an agency of the United States Government might feel coerced into paying —even a wrongful debt. It is illegal for private collection agencies to use any official-sounding name, letterhead, or envelope which would mislead a debtor to believe the collector is associated with the federal government. Apparently, however, there is no rule against the use of a genuine U.S. Government letterhead on behalf of private lenders seeking to collect debts. Not surprisingly, the FHA has found its preclaim letter "amazingly successful: 55 per cent of all delinquent accounts where the letter is used are paid in full or made active again."

The preclaim letter sent to Monarch victims:

[*United States Seal*]

United States of America — *Title I Collections*

Federal Housing Administration

Dear________: *Re: Your Title I loan with:*

____

We have been informed by the above financial institution that your home-improvement loan obtained under the provisions of Title I of the National Housing Act is in a seriously delinquent condition.

The holder of your note is entitled to file claim for loss and assign the same to the United States Government for collection. The institution has notified us that it intends to take this action unless you make immediate arrangements to bring the account into satisfactory condition.

We strongly urge that you get in touch with officials of the institution at once and work out an acceptable payment program so that it will not be necessary for the Federal Government to assume responsibility for collecting this debt directly from you.

You are requested not to communicate with nor to send your remittance to the Federal Housing Administration. . . .

Sincerely,

Title I Representative

The FHA also encourages lenders to "pursue an aggressive policy in the collection of FHA property-improvement loans." As attorney John Rigby of Arnold & Porter, who handled some Monarch cases on a *pro bono* basis, points out: "The FHA by refusing to make good on FHA insurance until the lending institution has followed up every possible avenue of collection provides a built-in incentive for the lenders to be harsh in collection." According to FHA regulations, before a lender such as Citizens can claim FHA insurance on a defaulted debt, it must "exhaust all collection efforts," which may include litigation. The FHA urges lenders to use "form notices, dictated letters, telegrams, telephone calls, and personal contacts," and if warranted, an outside collection attorney, for the lender can also claim reimbursement for legal fees. In the case of Monarch, however, the FHA has paid no insurance claims because of irregularities. The institutions that took the FHA-insured mortagages from Monarch were left to their own devices to collect.

FHA officials have also refused to cooperate with Washington attorneys representing victims who were defrauded by the FHA-guaranteed loans. FHA officials, for example, have flatly denied to Neighborhood Legal Services lawyers, seeking proof of Monarch's overpricing, that any FHA appraisals of the value of Monarch's towne house front were ever made.

> *What rules for granting consumer credit [FHA-insured loans] should a good lending institution use?*
>
> *1. Consumer credit is intended to serve the buyer rather than the producer. 2. Consumer credit should be granted on a sound basis to create an asset and not a liability. 3. Consumer credit should be sold on a common-sense basis. 4. Consumer credit should be extended in accordance with the accepted code of ethics perfected by individuals and the banking profession. 5. The lender should determine the full obligations of the borrowers so his credit will not be overextended. 6. Good consumer credit builds character in the borrower; it does not destroy it.*
>
> —*Roy F. Cooke, then assistant commissioner of the Federal Housing Administration in a speech to bankers.*

STOVER LEE SHAW: Why do I owe them? What is the money for is the main thing I'm trying to find out. That's what I don't understand. Do you know?

IRVING TURNER, *attorney for Citizens Building and Loan Association, who was taking Shaw's deposition*: Do you know of any reason that the Building Association should not get paid. . . ?

SHAW: I feel they should have their money.

TURNER: Sir?

SHAW: I feel they should have their money.

TURNER: Yes?

SHAW: But they should collect it from the man who got it—Mr. Cohen. That man took that money, used it for himself. I never used a dime of that. And not toward my house, none of that there.

TURNER: Is there anything else you want to tell us about your defense in this case, Mr. Shaw?

SHAW: Well, all I want, mister, is justice.

TURNER: Sir?

SHAW: All I'm trying—looking for—is justice, that's all. If I'd made that loan with them people, you wouldn't have had no squawk from me. I'd have paid.

Shaw paid anyway. He paid $3686 plus $553.01 in attorney's fees for overpriced work that was never completed to an institution he had never heard of before he received a payment book for his FHA-insured loan. He paid because the court said he must because his signature was on a promissory note sold to Citizens, though neither Shaw nor his wife knowingly signed it.

In some instances customers who signed contracts with Monarch realized they were being cheated and tried to back out before signing promissory notes and mortgages. It was Monarch's practice then to take out mechanics' liens on their homes, which apparently frightened some into assenting to the work. In 1965 between January 6 and October 6 Monarch filed 101 intent-to-hold mechanics' liens, which was about 12 per cent of all the mechanics' liens filed that year in Washington's U.S. District Court.

The liens were filed by Monarch's attorney, Margaret Haywood, who also in December 1964 started collection suits. Between that time and February 1967, she filed thirty suits in General Sessions Court (now Superior Court), usually for breach of contract. As Monarch's lawyer she sued: George and Edna Jackson; Minnie Stewart and her son and daughter; Alexander Stewart and Dorothy Clayburn; Martha H. Jackson, a seventy-three-year-old widow who believed she had signed to let Monarch change the lock on her door and sand her floors; Adell Dark, a working mother with three small children; Norman E. and Cornelia Morris; Irene Beard, an elderly widow; Daniel and Della Wright; James and Ethel Fitzhugh; Emma Jimerson; Mary Meeks; Emma D. and Bernard Brooks; Evelyn E. Brent; Robert and Dorothy Cherry; Rhoda Duncan; Willis and Palace Davis; Frank J. and Mary Groschelle; Joseph and Hazel Hines; Maggie M. Lacy; Raymond D. and Rose Phillips; George and Mary Batts; John and Lillian Bonds; Thelma M. Harley; Mabel and Wardell Harrell, Jr.; Winnie Leak; Arthur and Dorothy Lyons; Alberta K.

Smith; Booker T. Judd; Edgar and Louise Kennedy; Zelma A. Burt; Zelmarine Arrington.

Some of the suits were lost by Monarch; others dragged on so long they were eventually dismissed. But in some instances Monarch was successful and people were obliged to pay, often for virtually nothing. In all cases Monarch held a mechanics' lien on the defendant's property, some lawyers said, as an intimidating measure to "coerce" homeowners to pay. Some were so alarmed by the lien, fearful that Monarch might try to enforce it and take their house, that they were willing to pay to get it removed.

An elderly Irene Beard paid $250 for "breach of contract" because she agreed to have her roof repaired and later found Monarch held a $3500 contract for a towne house front. Edgar and Louise Kennedy paid $500 to get the mechanic's lien released, although they say "no work whatsoever was ever done on their house." Minnie Stewart and her adult children made a court settlement to pay Monarch through Mrs. Haywood $3000 at $100 a month for a towne house front that was unfinished and forced upon them, the Stewarts say, through fraud and misrepresentation.

Robert and Dorothy Cherry, to avoid the cost of a lawyer, filed their own semiliterate answer in court after Mrs. Haywood sued them for $4000 due on a promissory note plus interest due and 15 per cent attorney's fees. "Dear sir i don't think i shuld pay when you did not do nothing but pant i am willing to pay for the pant because you did not completed in 30 days they house should be white But they pant it Red that is why i think i don't owe you no $4600." The Cherrys paid Mrs. Haywood $300 at $30 a month until August 1967. Zelmarine Arrington, sued in February 1967 on a promissory note for $9000, agreed to pay $2000 at $40 a month starting in January 1970.

Mrs. Adell Dark was forced to pay Monarch $625 for a routine spiking job. She hadn't wanted a towne house front; she had wanted the inside of her house fixed up and thought that's all she had agreed to. "I said I don't want anything done on the outside of my house because why should I pay $4000 to make a pretty front and the inside is fallin down." They had promised, she says, to "fix up the back porch and give me carpeting and fix up the floors and fix the ceiling and paint the walls." But one day when she wasn't home, Monarch's spiker came and put up some aluminum strips. She tore them down and threatened to sue Monarch if they touched her house. Instead they sued her.

When she went to court, they had a contract for an American towne house front for $5450 which she did not know she had signed. They also had a mechanic's lien on her house. Her lawyer, she says, advised her to settle without trial, so she did, and a judgment of $625 was entered against her. That amount might not seem high to some, but to Adell Dark, as to many others living on marginal incomes, it was a disaster. She was then working as a maid in a hotel, was supporting three young children, and trying to finish six years of high school at night so she could get a better job. To pay Monarch, as well as other creditors, she was forced to refinance her house through a new first mortgage with Perpetual Building Association for $9800.

Out of that she paid Monarch $625 and her attorney $250 in legal fees, plus, of course, closing costs on the loan. She also had to pay a contractor $4000 to repair the interior of her house after Monarch refused.

Mrs. Dark managed (she now has her high school diploma), but not without hardship, and she is still bitter over the injustice.

> "The lights was being cut off and the gas and everything. And I had no choice because I couldn't fight the case. I had no money. I had to work and take care of my children and myself and the home. It was a little bit too much pressure, first of all, just trying to hang on. There was no other way I could do it but to pay, and I didn't get nothing for it, and that's what made me so angry, but I took it. I took it well, but I still say it wasn't fair. It isn't fair. They said it was settled in court, but I say it was pushed out of court because I had no alternative. I had no voice because I couldn't fight a person that had give thousands of dollars and I had nothing. It was one of the dirtiest deals that I could think would ever happen in America.
>
> I just didn't believe a person could be so low-down and could do so much to someone who was just groping, trying to make a living. Those people just plain took advantage of people and should be punished. The lawyer for the other side—it was a lady, a black woman, very fair complexion. Well, I'll tell ya one thing, you don't trust anyone. I don't trust anyone any more, I don't care if it's black or white or green or orange, cause if there's a dollar bill involved they don't care if they hurt their mama, some people."

COHEN ALSO OCCASIONALLY sold notes to individual investors, and eventually, when the FHA financing dried up, he turned to other financial institutions, most notably Atlas Financial Corporation, a multimillion-dollar enterprise with headquarters in Philadelphia. Atlas bought seventy-seven notes from Monarch, most of them through a D. C. broker, John Morgan, operating as Bankers Mortgage Company. Cohen got the notes and mortgages signed in blank and then filled them in with sums necessary to guarantee the desired profit for Cohen and Morgan. The records of Atlas show that they consistently bought Monarch notes at a large discount. They usually paid him only 60 per cent, or 60 cents on each dollar of the face value of the note. For example, if Cohen was to realize $3500 from an Atlas-purchased note, it would have to be filled in for nearly twice that much, at least $6500. Morgan then received $3880 from Atlas, out of which he gave Cohen $3500 and kept a $380 cut for himself.

Because the notes sold to Atlas had to be so flagrantly inflated for Monarch to make its regular profit, those who became debtors to Atlas often found themselves the most shockingly in debt.

Ruby Perkins, an elderly widow, was formerly a secretary at the YMCA getting $39.50 a week and is now retired on Social Security. At the settlement conference Cohen told her the work would be $4500; she signed a blank note, saying she trusted him, and in August 1965 started making payments of $88.07 monthly to Atlas. She never realized her total indebtedness until one day she multiplied her payments to Atlas by 84 months and discovered her note was for $7397.88, some $3000 more than she expected. Monarch also took $3925 from her in a new first mortgage.

Dorothy T. Degering, fearful of losing her house to urban renewal, signed papers with Monarch and later found that Atlas held her note for $9000. In order to pay off Atlas, she refinanced her own home and that of her elderly father, putting her $23,000 in debt.

Monarch's customers who lagged in paying were subjected to a constant barrage of phone calls and letters from many noteholders. But harassment in its most systematic form came from Atlas, whose collection methods are well-organized and computerized. Its president has testified that Atlas spends $150,000 yearly for WATS lines throughout the country (Atlas does business in forty-seven states); the lines are used for dunning. As D. C. attorney Andrew Zimmer, who won a court settlement for a Monarch client against Atlas, says, Atlas bought the flagrantly inflated notes on a "see-no-evil, hear-no-evil basis." And like others, they tried to collect by harassment and legal action if necessary. Just as Monarch had the most respected legal representation, so does Atlas. The firm handling legal collection in the District for Atlas is Amram, Hahn & Sundlum, which is the firm of Gilbert Hahn, Chairman of the D. C. City Council.

*

The kind of persistent, irritating treatment debtors were subjected to from Atlas is shown in a series of letters between Atlas and Mrs. Harriet Lyons. Atlas holds her note for $5754 which she does not recall signing.

Atlas Financial Corporation
7320 Old York Road
Philadelphia, Pennsylvania 19126

January 30, 1968

Dear Mrs. Lyons:

Your remittance of $70.00 has been received and applied toward your account. However, this still leaves the December and January installments due for a total sum of $183.00, which includes accrued late charges.

As we have informed you on many occasions, we are not going to carry your account delinquent, and expect you to bring same current.

We are advancing our file until the 7th of February at which time we expect to receive the above-mentioned amount.

February 12, 1968

Dear Mrs. Lyons:

In our letter of February 6, 1968, we informed you that we expected to receive $114.50 to bring your account current. However, this amount has not arrived.

We shall not carry your account continuously in a delinquent condition, and demand that the $114.50 be remitted upon receipt of this letter.

March 6, 1968

Dear Mrs. Lyons:

In our letter of February 23, 1968, we informed you that after receiving your payment of $75.00 your account was still delinquent. However, we have not received the necessary arrearage to bring same current, and as of this date there remains due a sum of $179.90.

These constant reminders on our part should not be necessary; and therefore, we demand that the $179.90 be remitted immediately.

March 27, 1968

Dear Mrs. Lyons:

Your remittance of $68.50 has been received and applied to your account. However, this still leaves $95.70 due for the month of February.

In view of the fact that your March installment shall be due shortly, we must insist that you forward the above amount to us by return mail and future installments when due.

April 19, 1968

Dear Mrs. Lyons:

We have not received any money from you since March 21, 1968, and as you are well aware the amount forwarded did not bring your account up to date nor pay same in full.

There is still $164.20 due.

Is it necessary that we institute foreclosure proceedings in order to get paid?

Your neglect in regard to this matter will not be ac-

cepted any longer, and demand is hereby made that the above-mentioned amount be remitted immediately.

August 1, 1968

Dear Mrs. Lyons:

You have apparently broken your promise to pay. We cannot continue friendly business relations unless you keep your word and your promises.

If payment is not already in the mail, we must demand an immediate remittance of $105.60.

October 22, 1969

Dear Mrs. Lyons:

As of this writing, your account is two payments in arrears. In cases such as this, we automatically refer the account to our attorney to proceed with the necessary action to collect the entire balance.

Rather than have to go to this extreme, we request that you immediately bring your account up to date with a payment of $228.80.

July 24, 1970

Dear Mrs. Lyons:

This will acknowledge receipt of your recent remittance of $205.50. This figure was applied to your January through March 30th installments and your account is now due for April 30, 1970, through June 30, 1970, in the amount of $174.00.

At this time I would like to know your future plan of payment on this account so that my records may be advanced accordingly. I would appreciate your speedy reply in answer to this request.

January 20, 1970

President
Atlas Financial Corp.
Philadelphia, Pa.
Dear Sir:

This letter is addressed to you in hopes that perhaps you are unaware of the methods used by one of your employees—J. J. Kramer in particular. Evidently he was assigned to my account for collection, but his method, as far as I am concerned, is very negative and his antagonizing ways do not encourage me in any *way to cooperate with your company.*

I realize that every financial institution desires all of its accounts to be current, but this is not always possible. It seems that I am always a little over a month in arrears and each time I have tried to catch up [which is difficult when you are on a fixed salary] it seems to be impossible, but I pay as often as I am able to. Mr. Kramer has talked to me (he calls three or four times a week) and I have given him a date on which I promise to send a payment. Almost invariably he calls back before the date on which I have said I would mail the check.

He has absolutely no business calling me either at my office or at home and leaving personal detailed messages about my finances with any person other than me. He has done this often. This is strictly unethical and makes me even less willing to attempt to get the account current because of his nasty attitude and harassing ways.

For several years I have been under the care of a physician for hypertensive heart disease which has been aggravated and intensified because of your Mr. Kramer. Anybody with any *common sense knows that constant stress and malicious harassment can only aggravate my condition. Evidently Mr. Kramer cannot understand this, but I am sure you realize that if his constant stress causes me to have a stroke or have to retire on disability, my financial condition is threatened and collection will be more difficult.*

Within the last six months I have been confined to bed at least three times because of excessive elevation of my blood pressure. I am also susceptible to upper respiratory ailments and have had two bouts of influenza within the last month. *All of this can be corroborated by my personal physician if necessary. I have spent over $50 for medicine and medical care this month.*

Meanwhile, during these times when Mr. Kramer called work and found I was not there, he has continuously called my home and harassed and insulted the lady (who is no relation to me) who has been taking care of me and answering the phone while I was ill. She has told Mr. Kramer that I was too ill to come to the phone and offered to take a message. He was extremely rude to her last Thursday. He called her four times in succession before she threatened to call the company and report him. Neither of us has to be subjected to this sort of treatment, regardless of who owes who.

Sincerely,
Harriet A. Lyons

MANY PERSONS paid for years with little or no protest, believing they had no recourse, and saw their incomes sapped for enormous debts Cohen had put upon them. In some instances homeowners were burdened with three or four mortgages. Marvin Greenfield took some of these mortgage notes and collected on them until 1968, when he sold them to another finance company, which continued to collect until 1970. When Monarch eventually folded, the notes it was holding went to Jack Gordon to whom the company was so deeply in debt. Gordon, too, collected on many of the notes until 1970.

In many cases people had to pay not only the face value of the note but also interest charges. The notes taken by Gordon and Greenfield usually bore interest of 6 per cent, which added about $800 to a $3900 note over five or six years. The first mortgages taken by Jefferson Federal and others always required 6½ per cent interest, which over 20 years—the usual term—nearly doubled the size of the debt, a $9000 loan, for example, becoming about $17,000. This interest was a penalty of incalculable harm, especially to those who through the years had substantially reduced their house loan, only to be struck again with twenty more years of needless interest. For the elderly, such loans became a sorrowful debt which they could not see discharged in their lifetime.

Bessie Burton, seventy-two, a widow living on Social Security of $91, spent nearly all her income on two mortgages arranged by Monarch, one held by Greenfield, and most of it went for interest. After seven years of paying she still owes $5000 on a first mortgage, and says she depends on money from her grandchildren to help her out.

Mrs. Eula Samson, an elderly woman who couldn't read well and thought she was signing a note for $900 which turned out to be $9000, had to cash in her insurance policies and those of her three daughters to pay the debt. Finally her daughter and daughter's husband had to move into the house and help her pay.

Edward Reddick, a man with seven children, thought his towne house front would cost $4000. Months later he realized he was committed to a first mortgage of $10,500 and a $9000 note held by Greenfield. By late 1970 he had paid a total of $12,000 on the two notes. Records from Towne House Construction Corporation show that the cost of the work was $1211.70.

Mary and Roy Gray ended up with four mortgages: one for $10,000 with Jefferson Federal, one with Citizens for $4337.42, a third for $4931 with Atlas, and a fourth for $1483 which went to Jack Gordon, a total indebtedness of $20,751.42. They paid faithfully on the last three mortgages until late 1970 when they stopped on the advice of their lawyer. They are still paying the first mortgage. Altogether they paid $9000 for a towne house front. Mr. Gray is a chauffeur at the Department of Commerce.

Emma Wood and her husband, who is now dead, incurred through Monarch a first mortgage of $11,000 with Lincoln Federal Savings and Loan Association and a second mortgage for $5500 sold to a private investor, whom Mrs. Wood doesn't know. The debt is collected by American Security and Trust Bank. "After my husband passed away in '67 I didn't know how I was going to make it. And I may never get it paid off," says Mrs. Wood, now seventy-five and living on Social Security and an annuity from the Bureau of Engraving and Printing where she used to work. She says she was told that the man who now owns her note banked with American Security and bought it as an investment for his children.

For some the unexpected debt with Monarch generated more and worse debt as those unable to pay became prey to loan sharks and other exploitative financing firms. Lettie Moore, who says she is "an old lady who was made a fool of," owed Monarch $4500 when she heard of a firm in Silver Spring willing to consolidate her debts. This firm induced her to sign a new first mortage for $12,500, a second mortgage note for $6200, and a third mortgage note for $4500, putting her in debt for $23,000. Helpless and confused, she explains regretfully: "Just think, if I hadn't met those Monarch people, this house would be bought and paid for. Now it takes everything I have."

MANY PAID only under extreme protest and economic duress, and in time became so weary they simply stopped paying and waited for the consequences.

Cora Blalock, then a widow of fifty-three, now remarried, is a minister in a small church she owns—"the Greater Emanuel Heavenly Mansion, a little mission on West Virginia Avenue, not a big place, just a house turned into a church on the first floor." In November 1964, when a Monarch salesman approached her—she says he was called Pops (most likely Daniel Pope)—her income came from renting out an apartment in another house she owned and occasionally doing day work. When the salesman told her her house would be condemned if she didn't fix it up, she believed him. When Cohen told her she was signing a "construction permit," she believed him. When they said the price wouldn't be over $2000, she believed them.

On January 31, 1965, she received a payment book from Citizens Building and Loan Association for $4337. "And I called the bank, and I called Mr. Cohen, and the lady answered the phone. I said, 'What's this price doing here?' I asked the bank, and so she said, 'Well, he brought the papers in here.' I said, 'Why didn't you all come to let me know something before you give him that money?' "

So Cora Blalock, as Citizens insisted, started paying right on time: February 20, 1965, she sent them $72.30. She continued for the next four months, but by July the drain on her meager income was critical. She was also trying to pay on a $6000 note owned by Jack Gordon which had suddenly appeared. Unable to make full payment to Citizens, she contacted their attorney Irving Turner, who urged her to pay something, as much as she could. She continued, sometimes $30 a month, sometimes $20. In July 1966 she could squeeze out only $10, a lapse that brought a reprimand from Citizens. Her letters to them, recounting her struggle to pay, are preserved in the files at Citizens:

July 27, 1966

Dear Mrs. Boyd:

Am sending $72.30 money order today which is one more month on my account. I do not want to get any further back because I want to pay my bill and I will pay my bill. My apartment was vacant ever since June 1965 and my place was not rented after that. And I told Mr. Cole when I get my place rented I would pay the full amount on my bill and I do not understand why all this came up, since Mr. Cole and I had an understanding about the bill that my apartment had to be fixed up with a frigidaire painted and everything had to be done to it. I will pay all the back notes. I do not want to owe anyone. I am still trying to get someone to pay it off for me, but it takes time to get in a business like that. Please send me a bill for all the back payments that I owe. Thank God, I rented my apartment today. The Monarch Construction people surely got me in a mess. The work was not even finished. They were here four times before I let them have this job. And they did not give or send me a contract. But I blame myself. I am trying to get someone to pay it off for me, and I will let you know as soon as they do. I will *send my regular payment every month as my apartment is rented.*

Thanking you in advance,
Mrs. Cora Blalock

December 20, 1966

Lawyer Irving Turner
Dear Sir:

I am writing to tell you about my problem with Citizens Bldg. and Loan Ass'n. I had promised you I would pay $100.00 a month. I did pay $100.00 for three months, but the weather has gotten cold now, and I have to pay for the heat. So please let me go until the spring of the year, and as soon as the heat is cut off I will start paying that $100.00 again. But now I can only pay $72.30 each month. I just sent $72.30 tonight and I will be sending that the 20th of every month as it is due on the 21st of each month and they will surely get that, because I am a widow and I have no one to help me. My daughter has 8 children and they cannot help me at all. I do thank you if you will do this for me. May God bless you.

Sincerely,
Mrs. Cora Blalock
Merry Christmas and a Happy New Year to you.

October 9, 1967

Citizens Bldg. & Loan Assn
Sirs,

Am forwarding $30.00 on bill this month. This is the best I can do for now because my apartments were not rented out as my place was so badly destroyed and broken up that I had to take my money to get it back in decent shape to rent. Mr. Cohen who fixed the house charged me *too much money, and that is why I could not pay you all more. I am still working on the apt. I cannot borrow any money from the bank as I owe you all too much and Mr. Cohen who took out the contract for the job charged me too much money for the work.*

This is all I can do now but as soon as I get my apt rented which I hope will be by the 1st of November I will be able to pay you $72.30 every month I hope. Thanking you for your consideration.

Respectfully,
Mrs. Cora Blalock

Nov. 4, 1967

Citizens Bldg. & Loan Assn
Dear Sirs,

Am not sending the full amount but I just want you to know that I am willing to pay you but I told you I had to get my apartment fixed up over here and now I have finished it and am looking to rent it next week. The next time I hope I will be able to send you $72.30.

Mrs. Cora Blalock

Then Cora Blalock gave up. On November 27, 1967, she made her last payment of $50 to Citizens Building and Loan Association. By that time she knew she had been victimized, and she was weary and angry. The spirit of civil rights was also growing stronger, and she understood, too, that being black had something to do with being cheated.

"After I had struggled so hard, not a soul, nobody tell me nothing. I'm a praying woman, and I pray and ask the Lord to help me, see. I pray and I say, 'Lord, now you know this man shouldn't have robbed me like this. This was wrong.' I went to the Lord and I talked to him about it. Well, He say, 'Yes, it is wrong for him to do it.' So I stepped out and helped myself [by stopping payment]. That's all. I know it was wrong. God know it's wrong."

Citizens was not long responding.

December 27, 1967

Dear members:

Our firm has instituted foreclosure proceedings against your property.

Please have someone home on January 2, 1968, as we are sending someone to appraise your property.

We would appreciate your having someone home as any delay will only cause you further embarrassment and expense.

However, you can forestall this action by remitting all past due payments as shown below before the appraisal date.

Very truly yours,
B. A. Catalano
Collection Manager

Amt. past due: $289.20

"I went on and tried to pay, tried to pay, tried to pay, and I look at the house when I walk up my steps and I say, 'Isn't it a shame, I'm paying all that money, for what?' Just look at what I'm paying, just look at what I'm doing, for nothing. And I would call the bank and talk to the bank, and they would say, 'I'm selling your home,' and they talked to me like I was a dog in the street somewhere. I'm telling you the truth. That Citizens people sure had me like a ghost. It's a wonder I'm in the world today.

> I couldn't sleep cause of the way they were treating me. If you don't pay, we're going to take your house. And they would say ugly things, too, some of those boys in there. Sure did. . . . And I'm sick of it now. I can't hardly stand it. I know people like that cause I'm black and they's white they think I was a dog or something and they're going to turn me out of my house and all that kind of stuff. They think I'm a dog on the street if I don't pay them some money. . . . I've been telling you how I've been mistreated and how I've been robbed and everything and how I tried to do my best with the bank and talk with them and that they would help me because it wasn't right the way I was treated. I wish you could see the work they did on that house for what he charged me, I wish you could see it."

Cora Blalock obtained two lawyers, Paul Pascal and Noel Thompson, who in January 1968 filed suit against Citizens in an effort to prevent their foreclosing. In December 1971 the suit was still pending, and Citizens, despite intervening events in which Nathan Cohen admitted defrauding Mrs. Blalock, was still pressing for payment and threatening to foreclose on both her home and her small mission, where she takes in the homeless at night. But Citizens still insists it is a bona fide holder in due course and entitled to be paid.

*

Ida Stevenson, born in the mountains of Virginia, never got beyond the third grade in school. Her husband, Roy, now dead, never went to school at all as far as she knew, and could neither read nor write. He worked all his life on the construction crews in the streets of Washington. For twenty-four years, until 1968, she worked in a federal government cafeteria, in later years as a dishwashing machine operator. Now sixty-seven years old, she recalls that in May 1964 she came home from work and found her husband with two men—probably Nathan Cohen and Myrvin Clark. They had Roy Stevenson's mark—a large X such as a child might make—on a contract for a towne house front. They were waiting for Ida to come home so she could sign too. She didn't want to, "but they kept a-beggin' me." So she signed that paper, alongside of her husband's mark, plus other papers she couldn't have read had she tried. The papers bear the witness signatures of Myrvin C. Clark and Nathan Cohen. Some were contracts, undated, for $4900, $3500, and $450; others were promissory notes and mortgages on their house on 5th Street, N.E.

Later—on June 9—some men came and took them "over on F Street somewhere" early in the morning where they signed more papers; she remembers she was nervous about being late for work, so she hurried and signed. Ida Stevenson has no comprehension of what she signed or why; she knows only that it had something to do with "a house note, the place you pay for your house." This time, according to the records, Earl M. Lapin witnessed her husband's mark. Mrs. Stevenson says she has never heard of Earl Lapin, the broker to whom she eventually paid a $525 fee, purportedly for explaining to her and her husband the papers of the new first mortgage which he had negotiated with the Montgomery Federal Savings and Loan Association in Silver Spring. It was for $10,500, and the settlement sheet shows the loan was loaded with closing costs.

Loan: Montgomery Savings Assn		10,500
Fire & Extd Coverage Ins.	72.00	
Appraisal Fee	50.00	
Commission		
Conveyancing paid: Trust and Note	15.00	
First Deed of Trust: Equitable S & L Assn	4088.38	
Interest Accrued from	11.86	
Bonus—Release Charge	15.50	
Third Deed of Trust: A S & T, 8th & H NE	2344.00	
Interest Accrued from: May 1st	19.89	
Trustee Fee: 2nd Trust	20.00	
Trustee Fee: 3rd Trust	20.00	
Taxes Paid thru 6/30/64	61.80	
Taxes Accrued from		
Front Food Benefit		
Town Taxes		
Inspection Fee	15.00	
Pay to Empire Realty Service, Inc.	525.00	
Pay to Anderson Furniture Co.	271.05	
Service Charge to Montgomery Sav-Assn	525.00	
Credit Report	10.00	
Advance Taxes to Montgomery S Assn	90.00	
Pay FHA Note 7th & Mass.	35.27	
Title Insurance: Record Title	49.40	
Full Coverage	27.50	
Tax Report and Tax Service	2.50	
Preparing Deed: Releases	20.00	
Recording Deed	15.00	
Noting and Examining Conveyances	6.00	

Notary Fee & Notary Service:		
Trust Note	7.50	
Settlement Fee	26.00	
Registering Notes	5.00	
Revenue Stamps		
Survey Transfer Tax		
Pay to Monarch Construction Corporation When Work Is Completed	1850.00	
Balance to Borrowers	300.90	
	10,500.00	10,500

Seven months after the transaction, on January 15, 1965, Roy Stevenson died suddenly of a stroke. And soon after, Ida Stevenson, who knew nothing of what had to be paid (her husband had taken care of all the business), began to receive dunning notices from Montgomery Savings and from Citizens, which she viewed with incomprehension but blindly tried to pay. When she got behind, there were always the prodding notices from the banks:

Montgomery Federal Savings and Loan Association
Your mortgage loan is two months delinquent. The payments are due as follows:

Payment due April 1 (balance)	$15.00
Late charge for April	6.00
Payment due May 1	95.00
Late charge for May 1	6.00
Total delinquency	$122.00

The full amount as shown above must be paid immediately or foreclosure proceedings will begin without further notice. We will institute these proceedings unless the payment is received by [in four days].

This is your final notice. Call this office at once.

Citizens Building and Loan Association, Inc.
YOUR HOME-IMPROVEMENT LOAN IS SERIOUSLY DELINQUENT.
IT IS NOW NECESSARY TO PROCEED WITH THE FOLLOWING STEPS:
STEP # 1. TELEPHONE CALL TO YOUR RESIDENCE.
STEP # 2. TELEPHONE CALL TO YOUR EMPLOYER
STEP # 3. LETTER TO YOUR EMPLOYER
STEP # 4. SUIT AND ATTACHMENT
HOW FAR MUST WE GO WITH YOU?

Poor Ida Stevenson tried. "Oh, my gracious, yes, I paid them every month. I went out there—they called for me to come out there—I told them I couldn't pay, but they say, 'Missus Stevenson, you have to pay that bill.' Thank the Lord, they didn't make me lose my home. I said, 'I've got to live somewhere. I can't live out there in the street.'

> "It really is the worse thing that ever happened. Every time I turn around, there a bill here, there a bill. Oh, I had to go to the doctor a lot of times for my nerves. He give me medicine to take. I couldn't even sleep hardly when I got those nerve spells on. Then he said, 'Somethin pressin on your mind.' He told me to be quiet and take it easy. And I was singing in the choir—well, you got to give up something or other, so I give up the choir."

When Ida Stevenson retired, she got some retirement pay: $1000 to make her old age easier, but as she says, "it didn't do me much good." She paid almost all of it to save her house. She sent $500 to Montgomery Federal and most of the rest to

Citizens. To her it represented twenty-four years of cleaning dishes, but in the world of finance it barely covered the two-loan procurement fees she had paid: $525 to Earl Lapin as broker and a $525 fee, commonly known as points, to Montgomery Federal.

After retirement nearly all of her monthly income of $150 went to Montgomery Federal and Citizens. To meet house payments she took a part-time job caring for an elderly neighbor. The neighbor often gave Ida things, like clothes, for which she had no money of her own.

"I struggled along, just ya know, did the best I could." Still, she got behind.

> "They used to call me on the phone. Oh, my goodness, they used to make me sick on that phone. They used to call, them people, they say, 'You Missus Stevenson?' I say, 'She's not home, she's not home,' They'd keep worrying me all the time, so I stopped answering. They worried me to death. Early in the mornings, in the afternoon kind a late. A whole lot of time I'd sit right cheer and let it ring, ring, ring. I didn't know who's calling, I didn't know if it was my sister. When she called, I was scared to answer. That's the truth.
>
> "No, no, I wasn't intended gittin no lawyer—until I couldn't do no different. That's one thing. I always didn't want to go in the law hands for nothing. I like to fight my battle by myself. I was trying to live a life so I wouldn't have to be in the law hands. Trying to live, you know, a Christian life. But that time I had to go, but it really hurts me that I did. Because I ain't never been in no trouble with no law."

Finally, the threats were so persistent, the burden so great, and Mrs. Stevenson became so frightened about being put out in the street that her neighbors were able to persuade her it would not be wrong to consult a lawyer. She went to Neighborhood Legal Services, who advised her to stop paying Citizens, whom she had already paid $3100 through the years. Citizens acted to foreclose on Mrs. Stevenson's home, and in December 1971 the case was still pending.

Mrs. Stevenson, shy, in a faded housedress, sits in her dining room decorated with pictures of Jack Kennedy and Christian plaques—Love Thy Neighbor, The Lord's Prayer—confused and bewildered by all that has happened to her, unable to understand how after a life of hard work she came to live off the charity of her neighbors. She shows some photos of her dead husband, Roy, the man who couldn't write his name. "I'm tellin ya the truth. Somebody tryin to do right and live right. Look like some of em sometime get the worse end of it. That's the truth, seem like."

ROY AND MARY TURNER used to live at 514 14th Street, N.E. Now they rent a place a block away on Tennessee Avenue. They had bought the house in 1958 for $11,500. Much of the house had been paid off—about $7000 of it—so when a Monarch salesman came by in December 1964, Roy Turner decided to let them put on a towne house front. The agreed-on price was $3000 with a single monthly payment of $76. Several days later they met Nathan Cohen, who told them he had to rewrite the contract, that they should tear up their old one. The new one, he said, would be cheaper. Sometime later he called them out to Monarch's offices in Silver Spring.

> "When we got there, Mr. Cohen wasn't there, but this other man had the papers all drawn up and he said, 'jus sign these, you don't have to read them, cause Mr. Cohen has already told me so and so and whatever it was supposed to be.' I said I'd never heard of somebody signing something without reading em. 'Well, it's all right,' he said, 'cause Mr. Cohen has done so and so.' A little after that Mr. Cohen came in, and him and this man took these papers to the back. When they came back, Mr. Cohen says to us, 'That's all,' I said, 'Don't we get a copy?' 'No, you don't need a copy,' he said.
>
> So we went out and stood by the bus stop, and Mr. Cohen and another man pulls up there in a big black car and says to us, 'If you all are going home, we'll take ya home.' So we got in the car. He was talking on the phone

in the car, telling somebody to get somebody off his mother's back, cause somebody was after his mother for money. He said to us, 'There's something I forgot to tell you before you left that office up there.' And he has this little sheet, blank piece of paper, he says this has to be signed before the loan was official, and he jus kept insistin about this paper being signed, and I said, 'Well, it's a blank piece of paper,' but he told my husband and me to sign, so we signed it."

The Turners never saw Nathan Cohen again, but that one meeting set in motion events from which they were never able to extricate themselves. They discovered that instead of owing the expected $3000, they owed Lincoln Federal Savings and Loan $9000, Citizens Building and Loan $3010, and Security Bank $900 (on a third mortgage held by Monarch). At the time Mary Turner was not working, and Roy Turner was a caretaker at Arlington National Cemetery where he had worked for seven years, earning less than $5000 a year. It was a crushing burden, for they also had prior debts, including doctor's bills for their one child, a girl, now fifteen, who needs periodic attention for a blood disease.

Nevertheless, the Turners started paying, and when they got behind, a man came from Allstate Mortgage Company (owned by Marvin Greenfield) and offered to refinance their $900 debt. They ended up deeper in debt, owing Allstate $2950. They were now paying each month $85 to Allstate, $89 to Lincoln, and $50 to Citizens.

As the Turners fell further and further behind, they were constantly threatened by foreclosure. Moreover, they were subjected to brutal harassment. Roy Turner was called at home and, most disturbingly, on his job, so much so that he was constantly being summoned to the personnel office. Citizens' collection agents also sent intimidating letters to his supervisor.

December 10, 1968

Arlington National Cemetery
Personnel
Fort Myer, Virginia
Dear Sir:

The purpose of this letter is to ask your assistance on the above-mentioned obligation [Roy W. Turner, Account No: FHA #7-5141].

We are in no way attempting to use your good office as a collection agency, but would appreciate any assistance you may render in having this employee phone or visit our office so that immediate arrangements can be made for payment of the amount due.

The above-mentioned employee contracted a Home-Improvement Loan under the provisions of Title One of the National Housing Act. The note is in a seriously delinquent condition. Mr. Turner made a $50 payment, but his account is still 10 months delinquent. Our firm is entitled to file claim for loss and assign the note to the U.S. Government for collection. We intend to take that action unless immediate arrangements are made by the above-named employee to bring the account current.

Please accept our thanks for your courtesy and cooperation in this matter.

Very truly yours,
William J. Pachler
Collection Manager

At that time Roy Turner had already paid Citizens nearly $2000, and he tried to make small payments, but nothing seemed satisfactory. When the calls kept coming at home, some of them particularly abusive, the Turners had their phone removed. Then their neighbors began getting calls.

> "Every night they was calling those neighbors across the street and talking about what they was gonna do to us—they was gonna sit my stuff out on the street. They called the neighbors across the street, they called the people next door, all hours of the night, not only in the day, in the night, and they harassed us *so*. This man that called me this night, he got so nasty. Well, he called me a Nigger. He said, 'Let me tell you one thing, Nigger, if I had you in my state, I would fix your business, and you either git out or we'll sit you out.' And this was some man from Citizens told me this.
>
> And if you'd hang up, they'd just continuously ring back, ring back."

Roy Turner, then nearly sixty-two years old, a particularly gentle and religious man, who had worked every day of his life since he was a twelve-year-old boy in Arkansas, "doing no harm to anybody," began to show the strain. He couldn't eat, he couldn't sleep, sometimes he couldn't even talk.

> "They harassed him until he got sick. My husband had got to the place one time when he came home he couldn't even talk from them worrying him to death. They nearly drove him to distraction. And they was worrying me too. I was sick, my child was sick—she had passed out; she had low pressure and they couldn't seem to bring her blood

up, and they worked on her all night and all the next day, and I was going back and forth to the hospital with her—and my husband was comin home every night, he wasn't able to eat his dinner, and he'd come in and sit down and he was jus so worried he didn't know *what* to do. And when he'd get back to work the next day, they'd be callin again, they'd have him up in that personnel. I tell ya what, I got to the place I just felt like takin me a gun, goin out there and shootin every one of them, the *whole* group of them—Allstate, Citizens, *and* Lincoln—*and* Mr. Cohen if I'd a got my hands on him."

Instead Mary and Roy Turner decided to leave the house they had lived in for twelve years and give it to their creditors. One night they packed their belongings in a truck and moved a block away to a rented house. A couple of months later they read their house was being sold at public auction. And one day Mary saw new occupants moving in. "My husband got to the place where he said, 'Well, just *give* em the house,' and we just got out and *give* it to em.' "

Says Roy Turner, "They kept bugging and bugging and bugging me, and I just couldn't stay under that pressure, and I had to get out from under them, so that's the way that house—I turned it loose. I don't want it any more. I don't care what they do with it now, they can do what they like. I was trying to buy it, but after I found out I couldn't buy it, I jus turned it loose."

Lincoln Federal Savings and Loan, where the Turners had their first mortgage, bought the house at foreclosure on

April 18, 1969 for $1000. In late 1971 they still owned it and were using it as a rental property.

The Turners through the years had invested some $10,000 in the house which they lost. And even though they had given up their sole possession of any value, their security and the sum of their labor for 12 years, they were to find it was not enough. As is common, the bank, being the only bidder, bought the property for less than the existing first mortgage (which they themselves held); thus Lincoln did not pay itself enough to cover the debt, and, appallingly, the Turners still owed Lincoln a "deficiency" of $1780. They also still owed Citizens more than $1000 and Allstate Mortgage $2100. The calls began again. And they were threatened with lawsuits for the remaining debts.

Roy Turner had in January already decided to file for bankruptcy, so he saw a lawyer and learned that, ironically, even a man desperately in debt cannot extricate himself without money. The attorney had to have $250 in advance. So little by little Roy Turner gathered together the money. On January 16, 1969, he paid $10. In February $40, in March $40, and in July $60. But the proceedings he hoped would save him were not timely enough. He was still being badgered mercilessly on his job. Finally he was told, he says, that he would have to pay his bills or retire. (Civil Service regulations allow an employee to be fired for failure to pay debts.) In October 1969 he retired at age sixty-two.

In April 1970 he scraped together a filing fee of $50, and even though he was still short $49, Mrs. Turner begged the attorney to proceed.

On April 28, 1970, the petition for bankruptcy was filed.

Debtor's Petition

Roy William Turner: "Your petitioner owes debts and is willing to surrender all his property for the benefit of his creditors except such as is exempt by law, and desires to obtain the benefit of the Act of Congress relating to bankruptcy."

The court then took note of the possessions of Roy Turner: "He testified: Rents house, married, living with wife; 1 child he supports; no one else lives in house. All furniture in house is his. Some rooms without furniture. Living room, dining room, kitchen, two bedrooms. Living room has—1 suite, of davenport, circular affair, television B/W; couple of end tables; no lamps. Dining room: table and 6 chairs, small homemade table. Kitchen: stove and refrigerator belong to landlord; one bedroom: bed, table, chest of drawers, dresser. Other bedroom: same as # 1. Pots, pans, dishes, glassware, tableware, sheets, pillowcases, towels, etc.

"Never had an auto. 514 14th Street, N.E. was home he was trying to buy. Abandoned house because he could not pay for it. No bank account. Last employed at Arlington Cemetery, October 16, 1969. Has not been employed since October 16, 1969. Not employed on April 28, 1970."

It was nearly over, but not quite. Under D. C. law certain items are not exempt—for example, a television set—so if the Turners desired to keep certain of their furniture they would have to "buy it back." Roy Turner was bewildered: "My husband say, now we have gotten out of the house, now why should they take all of my furniture?" Mary Turner, then working as a shipping clerk in a dress shop, took most of her salary to pay $217 to save the furniture. Every Thursday she took $50, most of her paycheck, to the bankruptcy trustee until it was paid. Her husband's pension had not yet started, so they sometimes went without food. "We have sit there at night and ate biscuits and tea with nothing else."

Roy Turner, now officially bankrupt, does odd jobs and lives in the rationalizing world of the helpless. "They swindled me out of a whole lot of money, but that's all right. I ain't worried about that, all I'm lookin around is just to live. I'm getting too old to be fooling around with money. I'd rather give up everything that I got than lose my soul messin around with money, because money ain't gonna be here when I'm gone. I'm puttin all my trust in God now. Ya see, when you're in debt, you're not free. You ain't free as long as that you owe somebody, because somewhere down the line, the way these people crazy about money, they gonna beat ya down and not leave ya nothing. But I don't believe in that, I believe in lettin the other fella have some and I get some. No, oh, no, I wouldn't sue nobody to get it back. That's throwing stones. Somebody come and do you a dirty deal, and you turn and do them a dirty deal back, that's throwing stones for stones, the Bible say. I don't believe in doing something to a person cause he done something to *me*. If he's done some bad tricks, I pray for him. God'll take care. I ain't gonna harm nobody."

Mary Turner is less forgiving. "They drove him out of his job, and drove us out of our house. And this has broken him, I mean this has really broken his spirit. He said as hard as we struggled to get that place and tried to make a home and we had to get out. These people aggravated the very life out of him. What I don't understand is when a government can let this thing happen, let somebody fraud people out of their homes, what kind of government is it?"

IN THAT SUMMER of 1965 as Nathan H. Cohen saw Monarch disintegrating under the pressure of federal investigations, he and Myrvin Clark formed another home-improvement company, called National Research and Development Corporation, with Jack Levitt as president. But National Research and Development quickly failed also, and in December 1965 Nathan Cohen and his family (his mother also worked at National Research as a bookkeeper) moved back to Baltimore. From then on Cohen engaged in a series of what Levitt later called "Nathan's misadventures." Cohen during the next five years organized a number of companies in Baltimore, sometimes with the help of his mother and brother-in-law, Stanley Silver, and often using friends, such as Levitt, as front men: Real Estate Training Institute (training persons in real-estate selling), Baltimore Business School (computer training), International Foundation Consultants (a fund-raising concern), Computer Counseling, Inc., Creative Financing Corporation, Digitator, Inc., Converted Code, Inc., Computer Analysis, Inc., Reading Development Corporation. Most of them are now defunct.

Myrvin C. Clark also went on to a number of business enterprises in the Washington area, and in 1968 a company he ran, Allied Builders Union, received a $553,000 grant from the U. S. Department of Labor, plus $108,000 from the Ford Foundation, to train ghetto youths to repair roofs. Clark was recommended for the grant by, among others, Congressman John Dowdy, now a friend Clark often called on for favors. The Labor Department canceled the grant a year later after investigations showed that only five roofing jobs were ever completed, little training was accomplished, and that Clark, as sales manager, and six members of his family had received more than $33,000 of the grant. In 1969 Clark moved to California, where he became involved in a number of selling ventures, including a real-estate development and a foundation, formed by a former Monarch salesman, to rehabilitate alcoholics and drug addicts. Marvin Greenfield, millionaire and Washington entrepreneur, continued to buy notes and real estate, including a shopping center in Clinton, Maryland, and to make money.

*

Through 1966 all was quiet. Nothing more was heard of the investigation in the U. S. Attorney's office. Cohen assumed Dowdy had fixed it, and Dowdy let him think so. Then in 1967 a subpoena was issued from the U. S. Post Office Department for the records of Monarch. Cohen panicked and immediately went to see Dowdy in his office at the Rayburn Building. "Mr. Dowdy told me I shouldn't worry, that the last thing the government did before dropping a case was to give it to the Post Office. There would be no indictment, he said." If Cohen was reassured, he shouldn't have been. The case of the *U.S. vs. Nathan Cohen, et al.*, though progressing slowly, was far from dead. It was in the hands of postal inspector Jason Souder, an experienced investigator, who was determined to build a case not only against Cohen and the other principals of Monarch, but also against Earl Lapin (Empire Realty Services) and the banks which had financed Monarch. Soon after, at Souder's instigation, subpoenas were issued for the records of Citizens and Jefferson Federal Savings and Loan Associations relating to Monarch. It is quite common to prosecute white-collar criminals under the mail fraud statute, for it is one of the government's toughest, broadest laws and one of the easiest to get a conviction under, for the criminal need only to have used the U. S. mails or caused them to be used in furtherance of his criminal activity. James Hoffa, for example, was convicted of mail fraud.

Still, in 1968 nothing happened. Then in May 1969—three and a half years after Monarch had died—Nathan Cohen learned through a friend of his in Washington that the investigation of Monarch was very much alive. Inspector Souder and J. L. Tessier, a postal inspector working with him, had just sent a detailed report on the Monarch operation to the U. S. Attorney's office in the District of Columbia. The report recommended prosecution and listed 20 possible defendants, including:

Nathan Cohen
Thelma Cohen
Marvin Greenfield
Thomas Proutt
Earl Lapin
J. A. Rushing (settlement officer at District Realty)
Salesmen:
Myrvin Clark
Julius (Jack) Levitt

Daniel C. Pope
Lyle Von Wagner
—and
Jefferson Federal Savings and Loan Association
Citizens Building and Loan Association
Montgomery Federal Savings and Loan Association
District Realty Title Insurance Corporation
Empire Realty Services, Inc.
Roseanne Realty Company

The case, Cohen learned, had been assigned to assistant U. S. Attorney Oliver Dibble, soon to retire. "Scared to death" again, Cohen called Myrvin Clark, who made an appointment for them to see their benefactor, Congressman John Dowdy of Texas. Clark recalls that Cohen was especially alarmed about his mother. "Nathan said, 'I can't have my mother indicted; that's one thing I'm not going to do.'" But this time Dowdy reportedly replied that with the change of administration from Democratic to Republican he "didn't have the contacts" he used to. He told Cohen to "get a good lawyer." At this advice, according to Clark, "Nathan turned white."

Dowdy suggested Cohen call Washington attorney Hugh McGee, known to be a friend of prosecutor Oliver Dibble. Cohen went to see McGee, "who said I'd come to the right person, that he and Dibble were good friends, that they played golf together and were in Alcoholics Anonymous together." Cohen said McGee asked for $30,000, suggesting that some of it would have to go to Dibble. Cohen wrote McGee a check for $2500, "all I could afford at the time." Later, Cohen said, he gave McGee $500 to take Dibble on a golfing weekend. What

Cohen hoped for now was to stall the prosecution until the five-year statute of limitations had expired and he could no longer be prosecuted. If he could make it until mid-1970 without an indictment, he figured, he would be a free man.

In the meantime Cohen had been the target of several civil suits as Monarch victims foundered under the burden of paying and more aggressive young lawyers came on the scene. Most notable among them was Maribeth Halloran who came to Washington's Neighborhood Legal Services in 1967, right out of law school. She is, in Judge Theodore Newman's words, "a very, very bright lawyer, operating on the frontier of the law and actively engaged in trying to change it." Patiently she began from victims' accounts and intensive investigation to reconstruct the Monarch tragedy and to file a number of suits asking for cancellation of the notes and mortgages and the return of monies paid. Attorneys Paul Pascal and Noel Thompson, working as a team, also took some Monarch cases. And old Colonel Julius Herwig continued his investigation of Monarch and tried to track down Nathan Cohen in Baltimore, but Cohen successfully avoided all summonses. If Monarch's attorney, Margaret Haywood, knew where to find Cohen, she refused to say. She insisted that she represented only the Monarch Construction Corporation, not its former president. In October 1967 Margaret Haywood was appointed to the D. C. City Council by President Johnson, and she resigned as Monarch's attorney, giving as her reason "possible conflict of interest." Pressing payment on the fraudulent notes was then turned over to another attorney.

Cohen, however, did not have the opportunity to see

whether his retainer to attorney Hugh McGee would get him past the statute of limitations. By mid-1969 Nathan Cohen was in other trouble. Several of his companies, which sold public stock, were under investigation by the Securities and Exchange Commission. Cohen was accused of selling unregistered stock and failing to disclose his interest in the companies, among other SEC violations. A grand jury had been convened in Baltimore to hear the charges, and several of Cohen's business associates had been called to testify. From what Cohen heard, "it looked like everybody was blaming me," he said. Presenting witnesses to the grand jury was U. S. Attorney Stephen H. Sachs, a young determined prosecutor with a reputation for pursuing white-collar criminals. With possible indictments pressing for both Monarch and the SEC violations, Cohen decided to try to end his troubles by one final act. In return for immunity from prosecution, Cohen decided to offer prosecutor Sachs a bigger case than he had: bribery of a United States Congressman.

In late October 1969 Cohen called Sachs. "I asked if I could come over and talk to him. I said I thought I could help the government prosecute a very important case. But he [Sachs] told me that I was the subject of a very important case myself, that there was a good possibility I would be the subject of a criminal prosecution. He told me I should get an attorney."

Cohen was upset by the rebuff, but he persisted. Finally a meeting was arranged with Sachs. Cohen remembers his reception by Sachs as "very cold." Sachs was suspicious, and Cohen was reluctant to give much information, including the name of the Congressman, until he had Sachs's assurance of immunity. Cohen wanted immunity for himself and his mother from all investigations relating to Monarch and the SEC matters.

As one government official says, after Cohen told his story, "the wires were burning between Sachs's office and the Justice Department," as the deal was worked out. On December 30, 1969, the terms of immunity were laid down in a letter between Sachs, for the government, and Cohen. In return for Cohen's full cooperation with the government in prosecuting Congressman Dowdy, including appearing as a government witness, all prosecutions against Cohen and his mother for SEC violations between 1967 and 1969 would be dropped. And none of the information Cohen furnished the government about Monarch could be used against him or his mother.

But there would be no official immunity from prosecution for his activities with Monarch. Dibble had retired, and the case was now in the hands of assistant U. S. Attorney Seymour Glanzer, a tough prosecutor with years of experience in fraud cases, and he refused to give Cohen immunity for his involvement with Monarch. However, prosecutor Sachs assured Cohen that "should criminal proceedings be brought against you [in the Monarch investigation] and should those proceedings be terminated by a finding or a plea of guilty, the government will bring to the attention of the sentencing court in an affirmative way such cooperation as you have given the government." In short, Sachs would try to get him off easy.

It was not difficult now for U. S. Attorney Sachs to obtain Myrvin Clark's corroboration of Cohen's charges against Congressman Dowdy. For Clark, like Cohen, was no stranger to Sachs. Clark was at the time under indictment in Baltimore for making fraudulent statements to a savings and loan company to obtain FHA-insured loans for home-improvement companies of which Clark was sales manager. Clark was also about to be indicted in Baltimore, along with prominent Capitol Hill lobbyist Nathan P. Voloshen, for allegedly defrauding H.B. Hirsch & Sons of $20,000 by promising to "advance the business interests" of the firm through contacts with high government officials.

In February 1970 Clark came East for a talk with Sachs, and on March 19, 1970, a letter of agreement was signed between the government and Clark. Clark would testify in any prosecution against Dowdy and would plead guilty to one count of transporting a bribe across state lines. He would testify in the Monarch investigation, then being conducted in Washington by Seymour Glanzer, and, like Cohen, would plead guilty to one count of mail fraud in the Monarch case. The FHA charges would be dismissed, and in the event of conviction on any of the charges, Sachs would speak on Clark's behalf and recommend concurrent sentences. Thus, Clark too was able virtually to clear up four separate indictments—or at least obtain leniency—by turning state's evidence against Dowdy.

The government, which had let the Monarch investigation linger in the U. S. Attorney's office for fully five years—ever since Monarch salesman Robert Freed had contacted Alfred Hantman in January 1965—was now in a frenetic rush to clear it up, reportedly to wipe the slate clean in preparation for the prosecution against Dowdy. It is said an edict came from top officials in the Justice Department to hurry the case along and restrict prosecution to those who could be convicted quickly. Glanzer, who took over the case in December 1969, focused on Monarch's three principals: Nathan Cohen, Myrvin Clark, and Marvin Greenfield. Postal inspector Jason Souder, for one, who believed the banks should be prosecuted for their complicity, was "thoroughly disgusted" with the decision.

"You see, Monarch was a terribly important case to the community," says Souder. "For this reason: Our major premise was the fact that Monarch and all of these others [fraudulent home-improvement companies] are symptoms of a more malignant condition, and that is, the rotten condition of the financial community that will permit loans to be made at the behest of such fraudulent operators as Monarch. Until somehow or other we are able to dig into that and expose it, we are only treating symptoms."

Glanzer agrees that the officials at Citizens who dealt with Monarch "should have known something was wrong" and that "their role in this was disgraceful," but he disagrees that they should have been prosecuted. "I did not have a case of criminal fraud against them," he says.

As Glanzer prepared his case for a grand jury in Washington, Stephen Sachs in Baltimore was having Nathan Cohen wired up by FBI men. On January 20, 1970, Nathan Herbert Cohen, outfitted with a miniature tape recorder on his back and two microphones on his shoulders—concealed under his shirt, jacket, and topcoat—was escorted by two FBI men to the office of Congressman John Dowdy in the Rayburn Building. Cohen went in alone. When he came out, he had John Dowdy's voice on tape:

COHEN: Hi there.

DOWDY: How are you?

COHEN: How are you, John? I'm—well, other than being a little upset, I'm, uh, I'm in pretty good shape. Uh. It's been a long time. Snowing like heck out there, uh.

DOWDY: Yeah, that's what they told me—

COHEN: And it's slippery, you know. There's nothing on the ground, just a little bit. And cars are sliding and they can't get up the hills. It's, uh, it's wild. Have you got a minute to, uh, talk to me? John, uh, Dibble's gone. I don't know why, I, you know, I don't know except that I—I have a feeling it's getting hot over there again. And, uh—

DOWDY: Well, it's not, no, it's they're switching over from the Democrats to the Republicans is what they're doing.

COHEN: Well, we—put it this way. Okay, when this thing came, you know, we originally put it to bed back in '65. And, uh, then it came up again last year, and remember I came to see you and you got McGee. And I thought it was, you know, quiet again. Now I get a call from some of my friends that, uh, that they've been, you know, Justice Department's been talking to 'em, you know, and, uh, I called up there one day and I asked for Mr. Dibble, and they said he wasn't there any more. This is just the other day. You know, I—I panicked, I mean, you know, I (laughs) I got very nervous. So I thought maybe you could find out what's going on possibly. Uh, and see if there's anything we can do about it, you know. It's been a long way, John. It's almost five years, you know, it'll be five years in—in about six more months. And I think the statute runs in six more months.

DOWDY: I don't know what, but that's probably right—it's somewhere in that neighborhood, uh—

COHEN: You know, this Monarch thing has been, you know, like for years already, years and years and years, and just never seems to go away. It—

DOWDY: We got so damn much stuff that's worse than that now. I don't know why they—

COHEN: Why they keep picking on it, huh? You know, I'm out of the business; I'm out; you know, it—it just doesn't even make sense, John. Um. Well, I wanted you to know this, uh, the twenty-five thousand back in '65. That, as far as I'm concerned, that's done its job. Because, you know, it's four—four and a half years. Okay? . . . And, uh, I'm not worried about the old money, John. I'm not trying to say, you know, you owe me this or anything. I—really I'm not! I—I feel like you know you did what, you know, what you said you were gonna do, and this is just like an unfortunate, uh, boomerang, you know. . . . What do you think? Can you—can you find out what's going on? And—

DOWDY: Well—

COHEN: —do something? Uh—

DOWDY: I can try to. Of course, with the change in administration I've lost all of my contacts. I'll just have to see what I can find out.

. . .

COHEN: I'm really worried, you know, and I—I just got, uh—there's just a feeling of confidence, you know, when I come in here, you know, that—

DOWDY: Well, I hope that I—I hope I can do something for you. I knew we could before, but—

COHEN: Well, you did! I mean, you know, it—it went away, you know. I don't think it would have gone away if you hadn't a done something.

DOWDY: Well, I don't either.

*

On the eve of an indictment against him by a grand jury, Cohen came to Glanzer's office. Glanzer showed him a copy of the indictment, already written, and Cohen asked if he could waive the indictment and plead guilty to one count. Glanzer agreed, and consequently, on March 13, 1970, Nathan Cohen pleaded guilty to an "information" on one count of mail fraud, violation of USC 1341. An information is a prosecutor's presentation of charges in lieu of an indictment by a grand jury, and Glanzer says it is commonly used. "Why go through indictment charges—an information is much quicker. I also had in mind that he was cooperating with the government in Baltimore," adds Glanzer.

Cohen admitted he, with Clark and Greenfield, devised a scheme to defraud homeowners, to obtain money and property by false and fraudulent pretenses, to induce homeowners to sign documents the nature and character of which was falsely represented to and concealed from them, to spike jobs, to induce homeowners by false pretenses to sign additional purported contracts, deeds of trust, and promissory notes for the purpose of increasing the amounts of money homeowners would be obligated to pay.

He also admitted he misrepresented to homeowners, among other things, that Monarch was affiliated with a government-sponsored program of urban renewal, that failure to purchase a towne house front would expose homeowners to the risk of losing their home through condemnation, that Monarch would consolidate certain debts, that homeowners would have one monthly payment on all debts in an amount less than the total of their then monthly payments on all debts, and that he concealed from homeowners that their mortgages would be completed after being signed and for a greater amount than orally represented.

On March 19 Myrvin C. Clark also pleaded guilty to one count of a similar information. With Cohen's and Clark's help, Glanzer then directed his entire case against the lone hold-out, Marvin Greenfield, who had tried to disguise his association with Monarch. Both Cohen and Clark in April testified against Greenfield to a grand jury in Washington, as did former Monarch salesman Daniel Pope and a number of victims Greenfield had defrauded. On April 27, 1970, Greenfield, too, on the advice of his attorney, Benton L. Becker, pleaded guilty to one count of mail fraud. The maximum sentence each of them could receive was five years in prison.

On March 31, 1970, a grand jury in Baltimore, relying heavily on testimony from the two con men, Nathan Cohen and Myrvin Clark, indicted the white-hatted Congressman John P. Dowdy, the conservative from Texas, on eight counts of: conspiracy to obstruct justice, the use of interstate facilities to promote bribery, and perjury in testimony given previously that year before a grand jury in Baltimore. Clark was indicted on one count of conspiracy in the case; Cohen was named a co-

conspirator but not indicted. Congressman Dowdy asserted his innocence, insisting later that he was being "framed" as part of Cohen and Clark's scheme to save themselves. In an aside to reporters, Dowdy said, quite accurately: "He [Cohen] has finally got the immunity he was seeking."

THERE WAS A packed courtroom of family, friends, and interested observers on Friday, January 8, 1971, when Nathan H. Cohen and Myrvin C. Clark came before Chief Judge Edward M. Curran in the U. S. District Court house for sentencing.

MR. MILLER: If the court please, Herbert J. Miller representing the defendant Nathan Cohen.

COURT: Do you want to say anything before the court imposes sentence?

MR. MILLER: If the court please, I wonder if I may make a few comments addressed to this case because I feel it is a particularly serious case, but I feel that there are very substantial mitigating circumstances I would wish to bring to the attention of the court.

As the court knows from the probation report—at least I assume it has seen the probation report—this defendant Nathan Cohen was a member of the National Guard and was honorably discharged from the Army. He graduated from law school with honors and worked for a brief period of time for the Federal Trade Commission under their honors program.

When he became a participant in the Monarch Construction Corporation, the concept that I always had from reading the newspapers was that there was a substantial profit made by this defendant out of the operation of Monarch. In fact, he lost $10,000, his mother lost $10,000, and his income in 1963 from Monarch was $5000, in 1964 was $10,400, and in 1965 was $17,500. I know, as the court knows, that when a man stands before the bar of justice for sentencing, there is repentance and contrition, but I would like to submit to the court that in this case there is more than that. There is a history of concrete, effective steps taken by this defendant over the past year to attempt to undo the wrong that in fact has been done.

For example, he went voluntarily to the office of the U.S. Attorney in Baltimore, Maryland, over a year ago and agreed fully to cooperate with the federal government in respect to another investigation pending.

Secondly, voluntarily, if the court please, and without benefit of counsel, he came to the District Court here and proceeded to explain to Mr. Seymour Glanzer, who was head of the fraud section, exactly how the operation of the Monarch Construction Corporation was conducted. He fully explained to Mr. Glanzer how the alleged fraud was committed. He went through the files with Mr. Glanzer, and in fact if it were not for the cooperation of this defendant, Nathan Cohen, there would be no information currently pending against Marvin Greenfield.

Without any strings attached he also testified before the Securities and Exchange Commission, and he testified before the Grand Jury in this case, and as I say, worked long hours and very hard to explain to Mr. Glanzer precisely how this scheme and artifice was constructed and how it worked.

Now I could say that this is one very important factor the court should take into consideration in mitigation. I would like to bring to the court's attention a second factor which I think is extremely important, and that is the fact that this defendant Nathan Cohen has voluntarily made himself available as a witness in many of the pending civil cases in which he is a defendant as well as the finance company. And I believe the court is aware that Mr. Paul L. Pascal and Mr. Noel H. Thompson, who are representing several of the complainants who were in fact defrauded in this case, have written commending the defendant for his complete and full cooperation with the plaintiffs and commending the defendant for the way he has attempted to right the wrongs which have been committed. Now if the court please, all of this I think is exceedingly important, but there is one additional factor in this case which I think has to be heavily weighed, and I hope the court will heavily weigh this factor. In addition to all the other efforts to make amends this defendant has made, which I have outlined, he is willing, if the court please, to dedicate the rest of his life to making whole the damage that he has inflicted on the people in the District of Columbia who dealt with Monarch.

He is not a wealthy man. He is not even what I would call a man who is well off, but he has authorized me to state to the court he would be willing to file a petition in the nature of an interpleading, to implead all of the plaintiffs and law suits currently pending against Monarch and Nathan Cohen. And that he would in fact deposit a substantial sum into the registry of the court which would be a part of this action as an interpleader, that he would in fact make monthly payments into that fund and all of that fund to be used to satisfy any damages which a court should adjudge had been suffered by a plaintiff by reason of the action.

Now one of the problems with the criminal law is that many times the only way society can obtain its fair share of the defendant's life is to sentence him to incarceration.

I would submit to the court that here we have a way, and I believe it would be a new precedent. I don't believe I have seen this tried in any court in the United States. It would be a new precedent to use this defendant and his earning capacity not to languish in jail, but in fact to work and work to pay back those people whom he has hurt and defrauded. And, if the court please, he is not only willing to do that but he wants to do that. I would submit to the court this is the way that the criminal law can in fact be used to make whole those who have suffered, to make restitution.

One additional factor I would like to bring to the court's attention is that the defendant is a family man devoted to his family. He has two daughters and a wife, and he has the support of his mother. He has a daughter, if the court please, who is now nine years. This daughter has a disease only recently recognized by medical science. I have submitted to the probation officer a letter from a leading specialist in this particular field. This girl requires constant attention, and the reason is that if her blood sugar level instability is not noticed quickly, it can result in a convulsion and a relapse, and there can, in fact, be brain damage. This defendant and his wife have constantly, carefully, watched this girl because, as the letter from the doctor and the attached curriculum vitae would indicate, the doctor explained how closely this girl must be watched. It is believed this is another factor. It is one thing to punish the defendant it is another thing to place the girl in a position where she does not have the care of her father when she is going through this very serious crisis.

This defendant has been punished already, if the court please. First of all, he has been disbarred—and I must confess on the record that he should have been disbarred—and secondly, the long nights and hours of worrying about an investigation and attempting to work placed him in a position where he could not attempt to undo what he has done wrong I know has created much tension and caused this defendant much grief. His health is not good.

For all of these reasons, if the court please; because of his strong full cooperation with law-enforcement authorities, which as the court knows is really the backbone of law enforcement in this country, and where you cannot get defendants to cooperate with the federal government you cannot in fact bring the prosecutions that should be brought; and because this man has worked long and diligently for counsel for plaintiffs in the various lawsuits which are pending against him, and who has voluntarily admitted his guilt in these pending lawsuits and tried to help plaintiffs to recover against the finance companies and done an excellent job; and because he is willing, if the court please, to establish a fund paid into the registry of the court under the concept of an interpleader to make restitution to accomplish that which cannot be done in any other way; and because of the fact his daughter is in a serious health condition; I respectfully recommend and request that the court consider leniency and grant this defendant probation so that he may continue to make the restitution to the benefit of all concerned.

THE JUDGE: Cohen, have you ever been convicted of a crime before?

DEFENDANT COHEN: No, Your Honor.

JUDGE: Are you willing to make restitution?

COHEN: Yes, Your Honor, with all my heart.

JUDGE: What you did in this case was reprehensible.

COHEN: Yes, Your Honor.

JUDGE: To cheat those poor people out of their money. Under the circumstances of this case I think it is more important that those poor people shall be reimbursed. If I send you to the penitentiary they can't be reimbursed. I am going to impose a sentence of one to four years, the execution of which is suspended. And you are placed on probation provided you make restitution.

COHEN: Thank you, Your Honor.

MR. MILLER: Thank you, Your Honor.

*

JUDGE CURRAN: Clark, do you want to say anything before the court imposes sentence?

FRANCIS N. IGLEHART, Clark's attorney: Your honor, as Mr. Miller has spoken for his client, I too wish to speak for mine. In view of the seriousness of the case and mitigating factors I feel should be considered by the court in respect to the man I represent, I wish to state:

That Mr. Clark also cooperated to the maximum extent with the government in the investigation and prosecution of this case. He testified voluntarily before the Grand Jury and I believe his testimony was instrumental in the bringing of the information filed against the defendant Marvin Greenfield. He has cooperated to the maximum extent with the government in a collateral investigation of a case in Baltimore. Mr. Sachs, the U.S. Attorney for the District of Maryland, is in court this morning to verify the extent of that cooperation. He stands ready to continue to cooperate with the government in any continuing investigation in this area that may be desired and should be continued with.

I wish to speak a moment about his role in the case

myself. I have reviewed the facts in the case, the testimony, the reports of investigators, and particularly the postal inspectors' report, a very lengthy one, submitted to the U. S. Attorney here in 1969. I have discussed with Mr. Glanzer many times and he agrees that this defendant did not rewrite contracts that had been obtained from innocent homeowners who were defrauded, that he had nothing to do with the execution of the deeds of trust, and he did not attend the settlements, in at least some of which there was a failure to apply monies advanced by the lending institutions, as there should have been, to prior indebtedness under the debt consolidation figure. His role was not in a sales capacity; he was one of several sales managers and at times he was simply a sales representative on the street. There was no evidence that he himself actually obtained or falsified any particular deed of trust causing damage to a homeowner.

I think it may be of some significance that the very end of his employment—and he was an employee, not an owner of this business or a director of the corporation—he resigned his position in June 1965 and for a short period of time went out on the street simply as a salesman. And the company ledger shows many contracts with his name during the last six weeks he was with the company which I believe, if the court examines, will show were substantially within a normal and valid price range. I think this may be of some significance in the case.

Now, I submitted to the court yesterday material pertaining to his personal history which I trust the court has had a chance to review. He served his country well in World War II when as a junior officer he was in charge of the re-educating and re-orienting of prisoners of war in fourteen camps. Every report and every commendation in the files submitted to the court from those days shows ratings of superior in every respect.

He stayed in the Army until 1950, having performed peacetime duty with the military government in Japan. He feels this was the beginning of his undoing, because it was during that period a serious drinking problem occurred and led to alcoholism which after discharge led to many of his difficulties, which he has made great efforts to overcome.

In 1969 he moved with his family to the state of California where he is far removed from his former environment and is far removed from the home-improvement business. He has at his home in California four younger children, two boys in high school and a daughter, Julia, in junior high school, and a special child of the family, a son Wade, age fourteen, who is a severely retarded child and who attends a school for retarded children and with whom the defendant has a very close and special relationship.

His wife of thirty years is in court today. Last month she obtained a real-estate license in California in order to work with her husband and contribute to the family income by selling homes in a development known as California City. She is a semi-invalid and she has not had prior experience in real estate or in business at all. And if this defendant is to serve a prison term it may be almost impossible for her to really support the family and discharge the duties she has as a sales agent without his experience and his connection with the International Direct Marketing Corporation which now employs him and which feeds leads for prospective customers to buy homes there.

He is a man of no wealth and no assets. He is willing to do whatever he can to contribute to the plan of restitution which Mr. Miller has spent so much time in working out. He is willing to make an initial contribution to that within thirty days. He authorized me to say that if the court would give him clemency, he would continue to contribute to the fund in any case where his name would appear as a soliciting agent where a homeowner has been damaged for the extent of his commission in each case. And he would go beyond that if the court or probation officer should feel this should be done.

In conclusion, I would just like to refer to the standards relating to probation approved by the American Bar Association House of Delegates in August of last year. It is stated that the criteria for granting probation should be as follows: Probation decisions should not turn upon generalizations, types of offenses, or existence of a prior criminal record, but upon the facts and circumstances in each case. The court should consider the nature and circumstances of the criminal history and the character of the offender and available institutional and community resources. Probation should be the sentence unless the sentencing court finds confinement is necessary to protect the public from further criminal activity by the offender, or the offender is in need of correctional treatment.

I have known Myrvin Clark for fourteen months now. I have observed the physical deteriorating resulting from the strain in this case. I have lived with him and can vouch for the effect that this case has had on him and on his family. He has a brother and a sister and other relatives in the court today who are all aware of the difficulties and his responsibilities in this case. I ask the court to consider his role, the actual role that he had and did not have in this case, and earnestly trust the court will consider probation so that he may support his family, send his child through school, and contribute as he should to the restitution program that Mr. Miller has outlined. Thank you, Your Honor.

THE JUDGE: Clark, are you willing to make restitution?

CLARK: Yes, sir.

JUDGE: Well, I will say the same thing for you that I said to Cohen: it is a reprehensible offense, but I think it is more important that those poor people who were cheated be made whole again. I will impose a sentence of one to four, the execution of which is suspended. You are placed on probation for five years provided you make restitution. If you don't, you will go to the penitentiary.

CLARK: Yes, sir.

IGLEHART: Thank you, Your Honor.

CLARK: Thank you.

Both Cohen and Clark walked out, free men.

*

At first Greenfield's attorney, Benton L. Becker, a former attorney in the Justice Department, believed that Greenfield would probably get two years' imprisonment. To avert that, Becker had urged Greenfield to buy back a number of Monarch-created notes and cancel them. He did buy and cancel ten such notes and offered Jack Gordon $25,000 for the notes he held, but Gordon refused. Becker also had conceived a plan of restitution which he and later Cohen's attorney Jack Miller (former Assistant Attorney General under Robert Kennedy) had worked out with probation officer Joseph Gallagher. Becker had talked several times to Judge Curran about it, and by the time of sentencing Becker was certain Greenfield could either get probation or not more than one year. Greenfield himself was so nervous and sure of imprisonment that he kept up a string of telephone calls to Becker at home, asking among other things that Becker request he be sent to a certain wing at Lewisburg Penitentiary. After hearing that Cohen and Clark had been given probation, though, Becker was relatively certain that the judge would have to do the same for Greenfield, even though he had no leverage as a government witness against Dowdy.

On Monday, January 11, the day of sentencing for Greenfield, Becker accidentally ran into Judge Curran before court and voiced what he thought would be a clinching argument in case the judge had doubts: "It would be a terrible thing, Judge, for Marvin Greenfield to be punished for *not* bribing John Dowdy." Greenfield's sentencing was swift.

JUDGE: Greenfield, do you want to say anything before the court imposes sentence?

GREENFIELD: Yes, Your Honor, I am very sorry for what has happened, and if given any opportunity at all, I will do everything in my power to try to make restitution to these people. Thank you, Your Honor.

JUDGE: Have you ever been convicted of a crime before, Mr. Greenfield?

GREENFIELD: No, sir.

JUDGE: Are you willing to make restitution in this case, Mr. Greenfield?

GREENFIELD: Yes, Your Honor.

JUDGE: You know what you did was most reprehensible, along with Cohen and the other co-defendant.

GREENFIELD: Yes, Your Honor.

JUDGE: The only reason I would even consider putting you on

probation is because you are going to make restitution and it would help the poor people who were defrauded by you. You ought to go to the penitentiary—you know that, don't you?

GREENFIELD: Yes, sir.

JUDGE: The court will impose a sentence of one to four years, the execution of which is suspended, and you are placed on probation for five years provided you join in with Cohen and the other in making restitution in this case.

MR. BECKER: Thank you very much, Your Honor.

*

Marvin Greenfield's net worth on that day was $1.6 million. He agreed to pay restitution of $200 a month for five years, a total of $12,000 for the damage he inflicted on Washington. Nathan Cohen agreed to put in an initial $5000 and also pay $200 a month for five years. Myrvin Clark agreed to $50 a month, to go only to those persons whom he had directly sold.

On the same day that Cohen and Clark were sentenced, January 8, 1971, other criminals were sentenced in D. C.'s U. S. District Court House: Robert D. Suggs, 18-years old, was sent to the Youth Correction Center at Lorton, Virginia, for snatching a purse that contained $40. Said the judge in denying probation: "This is a robbery case. There is just too much of that around."

Lloyd Perry, age 24, was sentenced to not less than two years' or more than six years' imprisonment for grand larceny, stealing a television set worth $500, and is now at Lorton.

Christopher Franklin, Jr., was given not less than three or more than nine years for housebreaking.

The same week Marvin Greenfield was sentenced: Shelly M. Hardin, a girl age 20, was given imprisonment of ten to thirty months for attempted robbery of the Eastern Savings and Loan Association. She handed the teller a note: "Give me all the money you have in the draw. I have a gun so don't try anything." Edward O. Jenkins, age 20, was sentenced to imprisonment not to exceed ten years for holding up the cashier of George Washington University for $339.75. Joseph Tindle was sent to Lorton for eighteen to fifty-four months; he and a friend stole $215 in cash and $100 worth of liquor from a coin machine company.

JANUARY, 1972:

Nathan H. Cohen lives in Virginia Beach, Virginia, where he builds houses under the company name of Windsor Sales, Inc., of which he is part owner. Myrvin C. Clark is "self-employed" in California City, California. Marvin Greenfield is tending his million-dollar real-estate interests in the D. C. area.

Grant and Theresa Taylor, Monarch's first customers, are living in Fayetteville, North Carolina.

James Thompson is still sending his monthly payments to Citizens Building and Loan Association.

Ida Stevenson is still paying Lincoln Federal Savings and Loan.

Emma Wood is still paying American Security and Trust Bank on a $5000 note, owner unknown.

Eula Samson is still paying Jefferson Federal, as are about two hundred other Monarch victims.

Roy and Mary Turner are still renting a house on Tennessee Avenue.

Citizens Building and Loan is still pressing court cases and threatening to foreclose.

And Atlas is still harassing its debtors for nonpayment.

The FHA-insured loans terminated in five years, and Citizens' attorney Irving Turner says most of them were paid off in 1969 and 1970, and the records show that the majority of mortgages held by president C. Edwin Kline and vice president Earl Morris have been released.

A spokesman for the firm of Amram, Hahn, Sundlun and Sandground, handling collection suits for Atlas Financial Corporation, says seventeen of the Monarch-created notes are in dispute. Presumably, the other notes Atlas took from Cohen have been paid, settled, or are still commanding monthly tributes.

The institutions—Jefferson Federal Savings and Loan, Montgomery Federal, Lincoln Federal, Eastern Federal—which dealt so generously with Earl Lapin, doling out money to him and Monarch from the new first mortgages, are all still collecting and apparently have no intention of ceasing. Many of Monarch's victims—barring intervention—will be paying on these unconscionable loans into the 1980s.

In January, 1971, Maribeth Halloran of Neighborhood Legal Services filed a class action suit on behalf of all of the victims of Monarch against: Jefferson Federal Savings and Loan Association, Eastern Federal Savings and Loan Association, Lincoln Federal Savings and Loan Association, Montgomery Federal Savings and Loan Association, Citizens Building and Loan Association, Atlas Subsidiaries of Delaware, Inc., Jack A. Gordon, Alvin Steinberg (Capital Syndicate, which subsequently bought Monarch notes), Universal Acceptance Corporation, Monarch Construction Corporation, Nathan H. Cohen, Marvin H. Greenfield, J. A. Rushing, Earl Lapin, Empire Realty Services, Inc., Towne House Construction, Inc., District Realty Title Insurance Corporation, Maryland Casualty Co., and American Casualty Company of Reading, Pennsylvania (bonding agents for Monarch), and seventeen individuals, who served as trustees on the mortgages, including C. Edwin Kline and Earl Morris; charging that the above institutions and individuals were engaged in a "joint venture for the purpose of wrongfully generating debt."

The suit asks for a cancellation of all notes and mortgages created by Monarch, an injunction against foreclosure on victims' homes, and compensatory and punitive damages. A year later the suit has still not been certified as a class action by the court, and the damage claims have been denied. In the meantime, attorney Halloran advised her clients, numbering about eighty, to stop payment on the notes held by Citizens, Atlas, Jack Gordon, and Marvin Greenfield.

In August 1971 Maribeth Halloran also persuaded the court to vacate the five-year-old judgment against Jimmie Brewster and Lillie Jackson and to terminate their garnishment. Citizens appealed the decision, but it was upheld.

Nathan Cohen has paid $7000 into the court restitution fund, Greenfield has paid $2200, and Clark has paid $500. The court has impounded the records of Monarch, at the request of Atlas's lawyers, to prevent publicity.

And on December 31, 1971, the Honorable Congressman from Texas, John Dowdy, looking old and in ill-health, was found guilty on all eight counts, and later sentenced to eighteen months in prison and fined $25,000 for perjury, accepting a bribe, and conspiring with Nathan Cohen and Myrvin Clark to obstruct the course of justice in the case of the Monarch Construction Corporation.

AFTERWORD

MONARCH WAS A TRAGEDY. But a tragedy that is played out many times over in areas throughout the country where there are poor people susceptible to similar frauds. The names and circumstances change, the laws vary, but the consequences are much the same. As this book goes to press a new scandal has been uncovered in New York in which numerous blacks and Puerto Ricans lost their homes in a scheme involving FHA mortgages. It is a common occurrence.

Yet these crimes get little attention and their long-term effects go unconsidered, though it can be argued that the threat to society from these respectable criminals is infinitely greater than the threat from more conspicuous crimes.

Says prosecutor Seymour Glanzer about Monarch: "A crime like this strikes at the very structure of people's lives; it is long-lasting; it takes a toll day in and day out." He sees a great difference between a consumer crime and a street crime which is over fast, usually involves small amounts of money, and produces some trauma, though the victim usually recovers.

"It's the difference between having measles and getting over it," he says, "and having long-term cancer."

The social costs are also enormous. The courts are jammed for years in slow, cumbersome efforts to make some small adjustments for the victims. But the process is ultimately defeated by the same antiquated laws by which the victims became entrapped. Monarch—like other crimes of its type—will never be wiped away, despite the bold efforts of some lawyers. The great majority of the injured will never sue, or, having sued, will never recover their money; most will consider it a victory if they can hold on to their homes.

The figure of four and a half million dollars used in this book as the size of the robbery is probably conservative. It is based on 100 victims each paying an average of $4500 for a towne house front. However, the FHA report found that the average Monarch-incurred debt among those interviewed was more than $6000, which if true for others, would place the larceny at over $6 million. There is no way of knowing. If one considers the interest, particularly on the twenty-year first mortgages, many of which were unwanted and unnecessary, as part of the fraudulent costs, the figure is much larger yet.

Where did all that money go? Much of it certainly was dissipated in company waste—construction materials, salaries, overhead, advertising, and selling expenses—just to keep the company alive. There is no evidence that Cohen or his family or others within Monarch walked away with millions. Cohen has said he lost money on Monarch, and there is no evidence to dispute that. Whatever he got he probably took out and spent as he went along. The rest? Ironically, as is common in such crimes, it is not necessarily the thief who profits. The other money drained from the poor was distributed throughout the community. It went into interest, fees and commissions to noteholders, the banks, the finance companies, the title-settlement companies, real-estate brokers, the collection lawyers. Which was fitting in one sense.

For if there is a single moral in Monarch, it is that Cohen could not have done it alone. He had to have the cooperation of the community's noncriminal elements, in fact, society's respected individuals and institutions, to make Monarch succeed. Without everyone doing his part—the bankers, the settlement officers, the brokers, the notaries public, the legal profession, the D. C. License Department, the FHA—Monarch could not have happened. Thus, it was not the work of one man or even a group of corrupt men; it was in a sense an unwitting community project. If bankers would not buy the paper, if lawyers would not press unfair collection suits, if notaries would not corrupt their names, such criminals as Cohen would find it difficult—if not impossible—to operate.

The laws should be changed. Neither in the District nor elsewhere should a creditor be able to foreclose on a house without going through court. As postal inspector Souder says: "There should be some legislation requiring a court review with evidence that foreclosure is proper; these notes and deeds of trust should go through somebody in a position of authority besides the auctioneer." The FHA must take greater responsibility for the loans made in its name through stricter regulations and controls. It is an outrage that the U. S. Government should be a participant in such frauds. Most important, the antiquated "holder in due course" law which allows financial institutions to go on collecting on wrongful debts, should be speedily abolished throughout the country either by state legislatures or an act of Congress. Monarch is testimony to the destruction that oppressive legal doctrine can cause.

As for the District of Columbia, there have been some changes in the law which, according to Neighborhood Legal Services lawyer Norman Barnett, gives "limited protection easily skirted by the unscrupulous seller." But he believes Monarch could happen all over again—tomorrow.

It could happen. Almost anywhere. Where there are poor people, imaginative criminals, and onlookers who refuse to see or care.

Jean Carper
April 9, 1972

APPENDIX

A Copy of the Information to which Nathan Cohen Pleaded Guilty

UNITED STATES DISTRICT COURT
FOR THE DISTRICT OF COLUMBIA

UNITED STATES OF AMERICA
v.
NATHAN H. COHEN

Criminal No. 412-70
Violation: 18 U.S.C. § 1341
18 U.S.C. § 2
Mail Fraud

INFORMATION

The United States Attorney in and for the District of Columbia charges:

1. From on or about January 1, 1963 and continuing thereafter up to and including December 31, 1965, Nathan H. Cohen, the defendant herein, and Myrvin C. Clark, and Marvin Greenfield being co-schemers but not defendants herein (defendant Cohen and co-schemers Clark and Greenfield being herein referred to collectively as "co-schemers"), unlawfully, wilfully and knowingly devised and intended to devise a scheme and artifice to defraud

Martha Hazel Green, Eddress and Almeta Martin,
Norwood and Essie Thompson, Albert Murray,

Willie Jordan, Emerson Davis, Mary J. Gleason,
Ellsworth Harris and Elizabeth Tobias, Claude
and Roseta Slaughter, Cora Blalock, Philip
and Elsie Johnson, Eleanor Elleby, Ocia
Whitfield, Irene Ford, Etta Thompson, Louise
Smallwood, William A. Wanamaker

and divers other persons, each and all of whom were members of and constituted a class of persons who possessed and enjoyed a right, title and interest in real property, and are hereinafter referred to as the Homeowners, and to obtain money and property by false and fraudulent pretenses, promises and representations the co-schemers knew would be false and fraudulent when made.

2. It was part of said scheme and artifice to defraud that the co-schemers would and did cause Monarch Construction Corporation, a Maryland Corporation, ("Monarch") to be operated and to maintain offices at 10111 Colesville Road, Silver Spring, Maryland from which address the co-schemers would and did trade as Monarch over whose affairs and policies the co-schemers would and did exert their control.

3. It was a further part of said scheme and artifice to defraud that the co-schemers would and did engage in an intensive sales campaign utilizing telephone solicitors and salesmen styled as "sales engineers" all in order to promote in the District of Columbia the sale of fronts for row houses called Town House fronts.

4. It was a further part of said scheme and artifice to defraud that the co-schemers would and did directly and indirectly by false and fraudulent pretenses, promises and representations induce the Homeowners to enter into purported contracts for the installation of town house fronts, other home improvements, debt consolidations and money loans.

5. It was a further part of said scheme and artifice to defraud that the co-schemers would and did induce the Homeowners to sign documents the nature and character of which was falsely represented to and concealed from the Homeowners.

6. It was a further part of said scheme and artifice to defraud that the co-schemers would and did prevent the Homeowners from canceling installation of town house fronts by making token starts on the installation which practice was referred to as "spiking."

7. It was a further part of said scheme and artifice to defraud

that the co-schemers would and did fail to leave copies of the purported contracts with Homeowners and would and did by further false and fraudulent pretenses, promises and representations induce the Homeowners to sign additional purported contracts, deeds of trust and promissory notes, all for the purpose of increasing the amounts of money which the Homeowners would be obligated to pay Monarch or its assignees.

8. It was a further part of said scheme and artifice to defraud that the co-schemers would and did cause to be certified by a Notary Public, an officer authorized to take acknowledgment of signatures on instruments which by law may be recorded, that Homeowners, personally appeared before them and acknowledged the signatures appearing on the herein mentioned "promissory notes" and "deeds of trust" to be their act and deed.

9. It was a further part of said scheme and artifice to defraud that the co-schemers would and did cause for their monetary gain the transfer of the herein abovementioned "promissory notes" and "deeds of trust" to persons and firms who would purport to be and would masquerade as "holders in due course" and who would collect from the Homeowners monies purportedly due and owing on the contracts, promissory notes and deeds of trust procured by fraud.

10. It was a further part of said scheme and artifice to defraud that the co-schemers would and did knowingly, unlawfully and wilfully make and cause to be made false and fraudulent pretenses, promises and representations well knowing at the time that the said pretenses, promises and representations would be and were false when made, including, but not limited to, the following:

a) Monarch was affiliated with a government sponsored program of urban renewal.

b) Failure to purchase a Monarch town house front would expose Homeowners to the risk of losing their home through condemnation.

c) Monarch would maintain and repair the town house front after installation for an unlimited period of time at no cost to Homeowners.

d) Monarch salesmen were "sales engineers" and were affiliated with the government.

e) An advisory committee of prominent local citizens reviewed, approved and oversaw each transaction between Monarch and Homeowners.

f) The total price which the Homeowners would owe pursuant to their contracts with Monarch was and would be as represented and stated to them.

g) The total obligations which the Homeowners incurred pursuant to the contracts with Monarch could and would be liquidated at the monthly payment rate which was and had been stated to them.

h) Monarch would consolidate certain debts of the Homeowners.

i) Monarch would pay or cause to be paid certain obligations then owed by the Homeowners as part of a consolidation of their debts.

j) The Homeowners would make only one monthly payment on all debts, including the debt to Monarch, which payment would be in an amount less than the total of their then monthly payments on all debts.

11. It was a further part of said scheme and artifice to defraud that the co-schemers would and did, knowingly and wilfully, cause to be and did fraudulently conceal from Homeowners the following:

a) The total amount which the Homeowner would be obligated to pay as a result of the transaction with Monarch was in excess of the amount which had been represented as the obligation which would be incurred.

b) The character and nature of documents which Homeowners were induced to sign.

c) Substantial balloon payments were required to be paid at maturity under the terms of contracts, promissory notes and deeds of trust.

d) Deeds of trust signed by Homeowners would thereafter be completed without authorization.

e) Deeds of trust signed by Homeowners when completed without authorization would be and were designed to obligate Homeowners in an amount greater and for a period other than had been orally stated and represented to Homeowners.

f) Deeds of trust signed by Homeowners would be and were recorded in the land records of the District of Columbia.

g) Documents bearing the signatures of Homeowners as thereafter completed would be and were transferred to third parties for money.

h) Monarch and its employees were not affiliated with any governmental program or agency.

i) Homeowners would be required to pay substantial fees and other costs at settlement.

j) Monarch's "sales engineers" had no professional training.

k) Debts had not been consolidated as represented.

l) Monarch did not comply with the Federal Housing Administration rules and regulations applicable to transactions with Homeowners.

12. On or about July 3, 1965, in the District of Columbia, for the purpose of executing the aforesaid scheme and artifice and attempting to do so, the defendant Nathan H. Cohen knowingly, wilfully and unlawfully caused to be delivered by the United States mails according to the directions thereon an envelope addressed to Stone's Mercantile Agency, 521—12th Street, NW., Washington, D. C. 20004 which contained a check in the amount of one hundred ninety-two dollars and forty-five cents.

(Violation 18 U.S.C. 1341 and 2)

Thomas A. Flannery
Attorney of the United States
in and for the District of Columbia